THE LAST FRONTIER FORESTS:

ECOSYSTEMS & ECONOMIES ON THE EDGE

WHAT IS THE STATUS OF THE WORLD'S REMAINING LARGE, NATURAL FOREST ECOSYSTEMS?

DIRK BRYANT, DANIEL NIELSEN & LAURA TANGLEY

A Contribution to the
Forest Frontiers Initiative

CONTRIBUTING AUTHORS:
NIGEL SIZER, MARTA MIRANDA,
PAIGE BROWN, NELS JOHNSON,
ANDREW MALK AND KENTON MILLER

1997

WORLD RESOURCES INSTITUTE

FOREST FRONTIERS INITIATIVE

DATA COLLABORATORS:
WORLD CONSERVATION MONITORING CENTRE AND THE WORLD WILDLIFE FUND

KATHLEEN COURRIER
Publications Director

Hyacinth Billings
Production Manager

Designed by:
Papyrus Design & Marketing, Washington, DC

MAJOR FINDINGS

■ Almost half of Earth's original forest cover is gone, much of it destroyed within the past three decades.

■ Today, just one fifth of the world's original forest cover remains in large tracts of relatively undisturbed forest – what WRI calls *frontier forest*.

■ Three countries – Russia, Canada, and Brazil – house almost 70 percent of the world's remaining frontier forest.

■ 40 percent of forest on Earth today qualifies as frontier forest.

■ Seventy-six countries assessed in this study have lost *all* of their frontier forest.

■ 39 percent of Earth's remaining frontier forest is threatened by logging, agricultural clearing, and other human activity.

■ Only 3 percent of the world's frontier forest falls entirely within the temperate zone (regions characterized by moderate climate, including much of the U.S and Europe). Today, temperate forests are the most endangered frontier forests of all.

■ Half of today's frontier forest lies in boreal regions within Canada, Russia, and Alaska – inhospitable northern zones between temperate forest and tundra.

■ Outside of boreal regions, about 75 percent of the world's frontier forest is threatened.

■ Eleven countries – including Finland, Sweden, Vietnam, Guatemala and Thailand – are on the verge of losing their frontier forest. These countries maintain less than 5 percent of their original forest as frontier, and all of it is threatened.

BOARD OF DIRECTORS

WORLD RESOURCES INSTITUTE

he World Resources Institute (WRI) is an independent center for policy research and technical assistance on global environmental and development issues. WRI's mission is to move human society to live in ways that protect Earth's environment and its capacity to provide for the needs and aspirations of current and future generations.

Because people are inspired by ideas, empowered by knowledge, and moved to change by greater understanding, the Institute provides — and helps other institutions provide — objective information and practical proposals for policy and institutional change that will foster environmentally sound, socially equitable development. WRI's particular concerns are with globally significant environmental problems and their interaction with economic development and social equity at all levels.

The Institute's current areas of work include economics, forests, bio-diversity, climate change, energy, sustainable agriculture, resource and environmental information, trade, technology, national strategies for environmental and resource management, business liaison, and human health.

In all of its policy research and work with institutions, WRI tries to build bridges between ideas and action, meshing the insights of scientific research, economic and institutional analyses, and practical experience with the need for open and participatory decision-making.

WORLD RESOURCES INSTITUTE

1709 New York Avenue, N.W.
Washington, D.C. 20006, U.S.A.
http://www.wri.org/wri

ACKNOWLEDGMENTS

DATA COLLABORATORS:
World Conservation Monitoring Centre, and World Wildlife Fund - US Conservation Science Program.

REGIONAL DATA COORDINATORS:
Conservation International (Latin America), and the Pacific Environment Resources Centre (Russia).

EXPERTS WHO HELPED WRI MAP THE FRONTIER FORESTS:

Africa:
Conrad Aveling (ECOFAC); Joerg Balsiger; Bryan Corran; Lee Hannah (Conservation International); John Hart (Wildlife Conservation Society); Illonga Itoua (World Wildlife Fund); Robert Kasisi; Dr. Nadine Laporte (University of Maryland); Jean LeJolly (Département de Biologie Végétale Université Libre de Bruxelles); Michel F. Massart (NASA Landsat Pathfinder Program/Central Africa); Aissitou Ndinga (IUCN); Simon Rietburgen (The World Bank); Nicodene Tchamou (IITA); David Wilkie (Biodiversity Support Program).

Asia:
Michael Green (World Conservation Monitoring Centre); Xiaojun Li (The Nature Conservancy); Kathy MacKinnon (The World Bank); John MacKinnon; Dennis Neilson; Evan Shield; Chris Wemmer (Conservation and Research Center); Tony Whitten (The World Bank); Eric Wikramanayake (World Wildlife Fund).

Oceania (including PNG):
Bruce Beehler (U.S. State Deptartment); Christopher Bragg (Department of Primary Industries-QFS); Gary Hartshorn (Organization for Tropical Studies); Don Henry (World Wildlife Fund); John Herbert (New Zealand Forest Research Institute); Jamie Kirkpatrick (University of Tasmania); Kathy MacKinnon (The World Bank); Dennis Neilson; Dr John Nelder (Queensland Herbarium); Stewart Noble (Environmental Resources Information Network); Evan Shield, Tony Whitten (The World Bank); Jann Williams (Centre for Plant Biodiversity Research); John Woinarski (Parks and Wildlife Commission of the Northern Territory).

South America:
José Marcio Ayres (IBAMA); Aaron Cavieres; Thomas Defler (Caparú Biological Station); Louise Emmons (The Smithsonian Institution); Philip Fearnside (Instituto Nacional de Pesquisas da Amazônia); Gustavo Fonseca (Conservation International); Robin Foster (Field Museum of Natural History); Rodolfo H. Gajardo Michell (Universidad de Chile); Gary Hartshorn (Organization for Tropical Studies); Otto Huber (Instituto Botánico); Rod Mast (Conservation International); Russ Mittermeier (Conservation International); Silvio Olivieri (Conservation International); Enrique Ortiz (Conservation International); Claudio Padua (University of Brazil); Carlos Peres (Universidade de São Paulo); Anthony Rylands (Conservation International); Jaime Salzar (Fundación Inguede); Stephan Schwartzman (Environmental Defense Fund); Wouter Veening (Netherlands Committee for IUCN).

Europe and Russia:
Dmitry Aksenov and staff (Biodiversity Conservation Center); Dr. Isaev Alecsander (Yakut Institute of Biology); David Gordon (Pacific Environment & Resources Center); Roger Olsson (Naturinformation Ab); Risto Paivinen and staff (European Forest Institute); Anatoli Shvidenko (International Institute for Applied Systems Analysis); Lisa Tracy (Pacific Environment & Resources Center); Boris Voronov (Institute for Water and Ecological Problems).

North and Central America:
Liz Barratt-Brown (Natural Resources Defense Council); Jean- François Bergeron (Ministère des Ressources Naturelles, Gouvernement du Québec); Dan Bullock (Manitoba Natural Resources); Chuck Carr (Wildlife Conservation Society); James Cayford (The Canadian Institute of Forestry); Rex Crawford (The Nature Conservancy); Barry Davidson (Wildlife Habitat Canada); Bob Demulder (Forest Inventory Development Group); Louise Emmons (The Smithsonian Institution); Robin Foster (Field Museum of Natural History); Tim Grey (Wildlands League); Randy Hagenstein (The Nature Conservancy); Mark Heathcott (Parks Canada); Harry Hirvonen (Environment Canada); Vicky Husband (Sierra Club BC); Laura Jackson (Protected Areas Association); Deborah Jensen (The Nature Conservancy); Kevin Kavanagh (World Wildlife Fund - Canada); Andy MacKinnon (BC Forest Service); Elizabeth May (Sierra Club Canada); Reed Noss (Oregon State University); Chris O'Brien (Ecology North); George Powell; Chris Shank (Wildlife Management Division, Government of the Northwest Territories); Jorge Soberón Mainero (Comisión para el Conocimiento y Uso de la Biodiversidad); Amanda Will (Protected Areas Association); Tim Wilson (Conservation Mapping); Dr. Ken Winterberger (U.S. Forest Service); Terje Vold (BC Forest Service); Gaile Whelan Enns (World Wildlife Fund Canada); Steve Zoltai (Canadian Forest Service).

Reviewers:
We would like to thank the following people who, in addition to the individuals named, provided valuable review comments and other input at various stages of this project: Janis Alcorn, Mark Aldrich, Kim Awbrey, Victoria Berry, Clare Billington, Susan Braatz, Louis Carbonnier, Domenick Dellasala, Eric Dinerstein, Yves Dube, Nigel Dudley, Lorene Flaming, Jerry Franklin, Mark Graham, David Harcharik, Rudolf Heinrich, Jurgen Hoth, Sue Iremonger, Klaus Janz, Val Kapos, Andrei Laletin, Jean-Paul Lanly, Claude Leger, Massimiliano Lorenzi, Richard Luxmoore, Michael McCloskey, Jeff McNeely, Norman Myers, David Olson, Jean Poitevin, Peter Raven, Kent Redford, Heather Rosmarin, Nick Salafsky, Jaime Salazar, Andre Savoie, Jeff Sayer, Peter Schlesinger, K.D. Singh, Bruce Stein, Tom Stone, Fred Swartzendruber, Frances Sullivan, and Derek Thompson. Within WRI we would like to express our gratitude to Chip Barber, Alan Brewster, Jake Brunner, Bruce Cabarle, Allen Hammond, Jonathan Lash, Mary Paden, Walter Reid, Leslie Roberts, Eric Rodenburg, Kirk Talbott, Peter Veit and Deanna Wolfire.

Researchers:
Steve Walters and Changhua Wu helped immensely throughout the initial stages of this report. We are indebted to them for their invaluable assistance.

FOREWORD

The word "frontier" conjures up notions of new challenges, of new lands, or new intellectual endeavors ripe for human exploitation and development. If a frontier is out there, people will not be far behind.

The frontier vision often saw trees as a commodity at best or simply an obstacle in the way of progress. Over many centuries, about half of the world's forests — almost 3 billion hectares — were burned, cleared, or cut down. Just one fifth of the world's original forest cover remains in large undisturbed tracts today, and the cutting has accelerated: about 16 million hectares are cut or burned each year. In the course of this devastation, we are losing species and a valuable cornucopia of resources, altering the atmosphere's composition and brutally degrading ecosystems.

Road building and other infrastructure development, often accompanying logging, mining, or other large investments, are also proceeding quickly. Once the way is paved, population pressure and landlessness in some parts of the world, especially developing countries, can prompt migration into frontier regions and rapid deforestation by small land holders and large land speculators.

There are better ways to use, manage and preserve forests. The reach of human ingenuity extends to the stewardship of trees, but at the frontiers the destruction continues.

This report describes for the first time the location and status of the world's frontier forests — the large, ecologically intact, and relatively undisturbed natural forests that still remain. Working with several partners, including the World Conservation Monitoring Centre, the World Wildlife Fund, and 90 forest experts, WRI developed a first map of frontier forest areas, assembling in one place unprecedented location-specific information on current and future threats to forest integrity.

Using a geographic information system, WRI has developed a single global database and a preliminary series of regional maps depicting the world's frontier forests — both first of their kinds. In the coming years, WRI will update and improve these maps and get their obvious message to the world's decision-makers.

This report is the opening salvo of WRI's Forest Frontiers Initiative, a five-year, multi-disciplinary effort to promote stewardship in and around the world's last major frontier forests by influencing investment, policy, and public opinion.

For each forest frontier region — in Amazonia, Central Africa, Asia, North America, and Russia — WRI is building a network of policy-makers, activists, investors, and researchers to promote alternatives to forest destruction that take advantage of the full economic potential of forests, not just immediate revenue from logging and forest clearing. As part of this effort, WRI will help build the capacity of local organizations to carry on this work independently.

The business community is an important partner in this effort. We are working with others to develop case studies with innovative firms to demonstrate the business impacts and opportunities that sustainability presents.

We must act quickly. Transnational logging companies are already operating in Siberia and Canada and rapidly expanding operations into South America, the Caribbean Rim, and Central Africa. Within the next five years, many pending and proposed contracts will be signed, and the leverage of governments and non-governmental organizations will be greatly diminished.

At the same time, mainstream industry and investors are increasingly open to change. There is a significant opportunity to increase market demand for "green" timber. WRI is already a backer of the Forest Stewardship Council, the first international organization created to evaluate, accredit, and monitor organizations that certify sustainably produced forest products. Meanwhile, many developing countries are searching for practical policy alternatives to destructive timber harvest agreements.

We are deeply grateful to the AVINA Group and the Netherlands Ministry of Foreign Affairs for their general support for the Forest Frontiers Initiative and to the Wallace Global Fund for supporting this project.

Jonathan Lash
President
World Resources Institute

INTRODUCTION

By now, most people who read a newspaper or watch television know that deforestation is a serious problem, particularly in the tropics. This World Resources Institute (WRI) analysis shows that we have lost almost half – almost 3 billion hectares – of the forests that once blanketed the earth. Every year at least 16 million additional hectares fall to the ax, torch, bulldozer, or chain saw. [1,2]

Hidden behind such familiar statistics, however, is another, equally sobering reality. Of the forests that do remain standing, the vast majority are no more than small or highly disturbed pieces of the fully functioning ecosystems they once were. These modified forests should not be

Hidden behind familiar statistics is an equally sobering reality. Of the forests that do remain standing, the vast majority are no more than small or highly disturbed pieces of the fully functioning ecosystems they once were.

forgotten, of course. They are the last refuge for some of the world's most endangered species and they provide important economic products and environmental services. Yet, they may have lost their ability to sustain themselves in the long term. To support their full complement of plant and animal inhabitants, fragmented forests will probably need regular interventions by resource managers.

In contrast, frontier forests – large, ecologically intact, and relatively undisturbed natural forests – are likely to survive indefinitely without human assistance. *(See Box 1 and the Technical Annex.)* Within these forests, natural ecological and evolutionary processes will continue to

generate and maintain the biodiversity upon which we all rely. Frontier forests also contribute a large portion of the ecological services – such as watershed protection and climate stabilization – that make the planet habitable. And they are home to many of the world's remaining indigenous peoples.

Keeping Earth's last frontier forests will require a fundamental shift in how we view them. From the American Wild West of the 1800s to Russia's Far East and the South American Amazon today, frontiers have been seen as limitless providers of land, timber, gold, wildlife, and other sources of wealth. Careless and wasteful, a typical frontier economy mines the forest for a quick profit and moves on.

We believe it is time to replace this outdated thinking with a concept of frontier that is based on stewardship – taking responsibility for the forest and ensuring that its riches will be available for future generations. Good stewardship may mean complete protection of some frontier forests combined with careful management of portions of others for both timber and non-timber products.

The change must happen soon: over the coming years, citizens, policy-makers, industry leaders, and others have a chance to decide the fate of the world's last frontier forests. The key decisions before us are windows of opportunity that may never open again.

WHY DO FRONTIER FORESTS MATTER?

As large, intact ecosystems, frontier forests differ fundamentally from the fragmented or otherwise modified forests that dominate the landscape today. For one thing, frontier forests are large enough to provide a safe haven for all of their indigenous species. To ensure long-term survival, far-ranging animals such as grizzly bears, harpy eagles, and wolves need blocks of natural habitat thousands, if not tens of thousands, of square kilometers in size. [3,4,5]

Fragmented forests, on the other hand, are probably too small to support their full complement of species in the coming centuries. [6] Smaller tracts are also vulnerable to processes beyond their borders. In the United States, for example, the nests of songbirds in small forest patches are under heavy attack by cowbirds, bluejays, raccoons, and other animals that thrive along forest edges. [7] Many non-frontier forests also lack the natural features that native species rely on: In the U.S. Pacific Northwest, the spotted owl and marbled murrelet – birds that depend on large, standing dead trees typically found in old-growth forests – are threatened by logging of these ecosystems. [8]

Secure habitats for indigenous species, frontier forests are invaluable refuges for global biodiversity. Between 50 and 90 percent of all terrestrial species inhabit the world's forests, [9] and many of them are threatened by extinction, primarily because of habitat loss. *(See Figure 1)* By maintaining these last strongholds we protect the biodiversity within them and provide a source for recolonizing non-frontier and restored forests with native species. Beyond its obvious intrinsic value, biodiversity supplies humans with food, medicines, and many other staples needed to survive and make a living.

More than safe houses for genes and species under siege, frontier forests maintain complex and inimitable ecological communities and processes. Vast and undisturbed, they give free play to nature and to such natural events as wildfires and seed dispersal by large herbivores, both of which determine the composition and distribution of species. Such natural processes create unique habitats, including ancient stands of "old-growth" forest.

FIGURE 1

Percent of the world's endangered animal species threatened by the loss of forest and other natural habitat

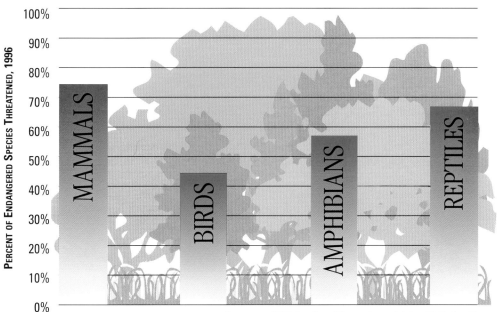

Source: IUCN Species Survival Commission, *1996 IUCN Red List of Threatened Animals* (IUCN, 1996, Gland), p. 36.

It is time to replace outdated thinking with a concept of frontier that is based on stewardship.

As large, intact ecosystems governed by nature, frontier forests provide baseline information on how such systems should work. Just as doctors use standard body temperature and blood pressure to determine health, ecologists study natural forests to evaluate the impact of different human interventions – asking, for instance, how forest clearing might affect local rainfall patterns. The results help land managers find ways to lighten the human footprint in heavily used landscapes.

All forests help maintain the environmental conditions that make life possible, from regional hydrologic cycles to global climate. But huge frontiers are particularly important. Frontier forest ecosystems store tremendous amounts of carbon, for example – approximately 433 billion tonnes, or more than all carbon that will be released from fossil fuel burning and cement manufacture over the next 69 years, at current global emission rates. [10] Without these forests, this carbon would go straight into the atmosphere as carbon dioxide, a powerful greenhouse gas.

Protecting and responsibly managing our last frontiers today will help countries avoid paying the high costs associated with massive forest loss and degradation. History abounds with examples of civilizations that foundered after deforestation led to soil erosion, river siltation, wood shortages, and other banes of agricultural and industrial productivity. These doomed civilizations include ancient societies in Mesopotamia, the Mediterranean, and Central America. [11]

More recently, erosion since 1950 due to deforestation is responsible for the loss of 580 million hectares of fertile land worldwide, an area bigger than all of Western Europe. [12] Loss of large forested watersheds is blamed for heavier flooding in India's Ganges Valley, and government losses of $1 billion a year in property damage. [13] By carefully managing what's left of the world's frontier forests, we can dramatically reduce such environmental side effects and costs.

Dwindling frontier forests are also home to many of the world's last indigenous cultures. About 50 million indigenous people live in tropical forests alone. [14] Amazonian forests house at least 400 indigenous groups – 1 million people in all. [15] Wiping out indigenous cultures by transforming forests is a moral crime. And when these cultures vanish, so does a gold mine of useful information about the natural world.

Frontier forests are invaluable refuges for global biodiversity.

A legacy inherited from our ancestors, Earth's last frontier forests may indeed be the most valuable gift we can leave for our children. Guardians of biodiversity, indigenous cultures, and ecological processes, frontiers also provide recreational and ecotourism opportunities. Because so many irreplaceable forests have already disappeared, the worth to future generations of those that remain is greater than ever.

Above and beyond practical considerations is the very real aesthetic and spiritual need just to know that remote and wild places remain on our crowded planet. One concrete reflection of this need is the considerable sum of money many people pay to visit such places. But even to many people who will never see them, wild plants and animals, along with the forests that house them, have an inalienable right to exist. Certainly, as Earth's most powerful species, we have a responsibility to ensure their survival.

WHAT DO WE KNOW ABOUT THE WORLD'S FORESTS?

Surprisingly, we know very little about the status of the world's forests as a whole. Most monitoring efforts are confined to individual countries, and the results often do not compute across borders.

Sponsored by the United Nations (U.N.), the most comprehensive study of the world's forests to date estimates recent deforestation, but gives no information on the overall condition of remaining forest. [16] This U.N. study cost $4 million – less than one eighth the amount U.S. citizens spend each day on newspapers. [17,18]

People need to know that remote and wild places remain on our crowded planet.

To help fill the gap, WRI asked the World Conservation Monitoring Centre (WCMC) to develop a map of Earth's forest cover as it appeared 8,000 years ago. The result represents the first detailed attempt to show what the world's original forest cover looked like before humans began transforming it.

The WRI map also shows current forest cover, drawing from an earlier WCMC map that provides the most comprehensive image of total forest cover today. Though based on the best available data, the WCMC current forest

cover map is far from complete. Many areas depicted as forested can hardly be considered forest. Some are heavily degraded by logging and other activities, while others are single-species plantations. A rough picture of where forests are is invaluable, but until WRI's assessment virtually nothing was known about their condition on a global scale.

TABLE 1

Total Area in Original, Current and Frontier Forest

REGION	ORIGINAL FOREST (000 KM²)	TOTAL REMAINING FOREST (FRONTIER AND NON-FRONTIER FOREST) (000 KM²)	TOTAL REMAINING AS A % OF ORIGINAL FOREST	TOTAL FRONTIER FOREST (000 KM²)	FRONTIER FOREST AS A % OF TOTAL ORIGINAL FOREST	FRONTIER FOREST AS A % OF TOTAL REMAINING FOREST
Africa	6,799	2,302	34%	527	8%	23%
Asia	15,132	4,275	28%	844	6%	20%
North & Central America	12,656	9,453	75%	3,909	31%	41%
Central America	1,779	970	55%	172	10%	18%
North America	10,877	8,483	78%	3,737	34%	44%
South America	9,736	6,800	70%	4,439	46%	65%
Russia & Europe	16,449	9,604	58%	3,463	21%	36%
Europe	4,690	1,521	32%	14	0.3%	1%
Russia	11,759	8,083	69%	3,448	29%	43%
Oceania (i)	1,431	929	65%	319	22%	34%
World	62,203	33,363	54%	13,501	22%	40%

Notes: (i) Oceania consists of Papua New Guinea, Australia and New Zealand

WRI's Frontier Forests Assessment

Most information on forests is scattered far and wide and buried within the walls of isolated institutions. Much lives only in the minds of biologists and foresters who are experts on a single forest region.

Most of the tremendous amount of information on individual forests that exists is scattered far and wide and buried within the walls of isolated institutions. Much of it lives only in the minds of biologists and foresters who are experts on a single forest region.

Working with several partners – including WCMC and the World Wildlife Fund – WRI wove together some of this diverse data, knowledge, and expertise. First we developed a preliminary map of "candidate frontier forests" – large forested areas with few roads or modern settlements – and sent it to 90 forest experts around the world. Using criteria WRI developed, ten to fifteen experts for each region commented on proposed frontier areas – confirming sites as frontier forests, rejecting sites, or redrawing their shape and boundaries. *(See Box 1.)* [19]

Experts also supplied information on the status of frontiers they identified – if and how these forests are endangered by development. They also answered our queries about future threats, specifying whether frontiers were in timber concessions or housed such high-value resources as timber, oil, or gold.

Using a geographic information system,[20] WRI combined all of these site-specific data into a single global database and a series of regional maps. *(See Maps 2-7.)* Far from perfect, these maps nonetheless provide the first realistic picture of the location and status of the world's frontier forests. In the coming months and years, WRI will work with partners around the globe to update and improve the maps as more information becomes available and to get them to decision-makers in whose hands the fate of frontier forests rests.

WRI's maps provide the first realistic picture of the location and status of the world's frontier forests.

DEFINITIONS USED IN THIS STUDY

FRONTIER FORESTS are the world's remaining large intact natural forest ecosystems. These forests are – on the whole – relatively undisturbed and big enough to maintain all of their biodiversity, including viable populations of the wide-ranging species associated with each forest type. As defined in this assessment, a frontier forest must meet seven criteria:

1. It is primarily forested.
2. It is big enough to support viable populations of all indigenous species associated with that forest type – measured by the forest's ability to support wide-ranging animal species (such as elephants, harpy eagles, or brown bears).
3. It is large enough to keep these species' populations viable even in the face of the natural disasters – such as hurricanes, fires, and pest or disease outbreaks – that might occur there in a century.

4. Its structure and composition are determined mainly by natural events, though limited human disturbance by traditional activities of the sort that have shaped forests for thousands of years – such as low-density shifting cultivation – is acceptable. As such, it remains relatively unmanaged by humans, and natural disturbances (such as fire) are permitted to shape much of the forest.
5. In forests where patches of trees of different ages would naturally occur, the landscape exhibits this type of heterogeneity.
6. It is dominated by indigenous tree species.
7. It is home to most, if not all, of the other plant and animal species that typically live in this type of forest.

THREATENED FRONTIER FORESTS are forests where ongoing or planned human activities (such as logging, agricultural clearing, and mining) will eventually degrade the ecosystem (through, for example, declines in or local extinctions of plants and animals or large-scale changes in the forest's age and structure).

LOW-THREAT POTENTIALLY VULNERABLE FRONTIER FORESTS are those not now considered under enough pressure to degrade ecosystems. But because they are unprotected and contain valuable natural resources, or because human encroachment is likely, most of these forests are vulnerable to future degradation and destruction.

NON-FRONTIER FORESTS are dominated by secondary forests, plantations, degraded forest, and patches of primary forest that do not meet this study's frontier criteria (even though some might be restored as frontier forest). This category includes some of the world's most unique, valuable, and endangered forest types, including the biologically rich, highly fragmented forests of Madagascar and Central Europe's last stands of old-growth forest. Such forests are high priorities for conservation. Non-frontier forests are also important because they provide us with a wide range of economic goods and services.

ORIGINAL FOREST is that estimated to have covered the planet about 8,000 years ago, before large-scale disturbance by modern society began.

A note about the data: This study's results represent estimates of the extent and location of frontier forests as well as threats to their survival. Incomplete information from some parts of the world and difficulties estimating the magnitude of threats make the data suitable only for regional comparisons and for distinguishing major differences among countries' forests. This study did not assess woodland areas of the world, or forests within many island countries. (See Technical Annex)

FALLING FRONTIERS

Nearly half – 46 percent – of the world's forest has been converted to farms, pastures, and other uses over the past 80 centuries. While just over half remains, most of it has been heavily altered by people and bears little resemblance to pristine forest. According to this assessment just 22 percent of Earth's original forest remains in large, relatively natural ecosystems. *(See Figure 2.)*

Of the remaining frontier forest that is left, nearly half is boreal forest. *(See Figure 3.)* A broad belt of primarily coniferous trees, boreal forests lie between arctic tundra to the north and warmer, temperate forests to the south. They blanket much of Alaska, Canada, Russia, and Scandinavia.

For two reasons, boreal forests have been less disturbed than have other forest types. First, long winters, poor soils, and other factors make farming difficult, so little forest has been converted to agriculture. Second, boreal trees, particularly in northern areas, tend to be slow-growing, scrawny, and widely dispersed. So until modern technology, increasing wood demand and other factors changed the picture, commercial loggers traditionally had little incentive to exploit boreal forests.

Temperate forests, on the other hand, are the most heavily fragmented and disturbed of all forest types. This study concludes that just 3 percent of today's frontier forests are temperate stands (another 5 percent contains both temperate and either boreal or tropical frontier forest). Thriving in a moderate climate, pristine temperate forests once extended throughout most of Europe, much of China and the continental United States, as well as parts of Canada, Australia, New Zealand, Chile, and Argentina.

Thanks to their favorable climate and fertile soils, temperate forests were the first to be cleared wholesale by humans. By 1000 B.C., most of eastern China's forests had been converted to farmland.[21] More than 2,000 years ago, the Greeks and Romans destroyed much of the forest that rimmed the Mediterranean.[22,23] Today, the frontier forests of the Middle East and Mediterranean Basin are completely gone. Western Europe's frontier forests were leveled during the Middle Ages as new cities and towns spread throughout the region.[24]

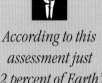

According to this assessment just 22 percent of Earth's original forest remains in large, relatively natural ecosystems.

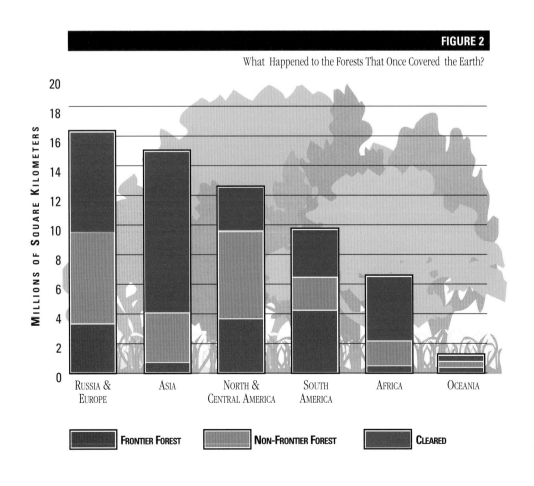

FIGURE 2

What Happened to the Forests That Once Covered the Earth?

(Vertical axis: Millions of Square Kilometers, 0 to 20)

Categories: Russia & Europe, Asia, North & Central America, South America, Africa, Oceania

Legend: ■ Frontier Forest ■ Non-Frontier Forest ■ Cleared

Temperate forests of the Americas, Australia, and New Zealand were opened relatively recently – over the past few centuries – by European explorers and settlers. Although indigenous peoples had long lived in and shaped these forests, newcomers wrought far more dramatic changes. *(See Box 2.)* Even so, almost all of the world's remaining temperate frontier forests are in these three regions.

The lion's share of today's frontier forests – more than 75 percent-is located in just three large tracts covering parts of seven countries.

Until this century, tropical forests – located in warm regions within 30 degrees of the equator – remained largely intact. In the past few decades, however, they have fallen with alarming speed. Between 1960 and 1990, some 450 million hectares were cleared – a fifth of the world's entire tropical forest cover. *(See Figure 4.)*

Millions more hectares have been degraded by logging, agricultural clearing, and the removal of vegetation for fuelwood, building materials, and livestock feed. In Asia and Africa, for example, this study found that though roughly a third of the original forest cover remains, less than 10 percent of this original cover still qualifies as frontier forest. *(See Table 1.)*

Worldwide, most frontier forests are now restricted to scattered, widely dispersed pockets, many located in inaccessible mountains or swamps. Europe – which has already lost two thirds of its historical forest cover – maintains only a few small patches of frontier forest totalling less than 1 percent of the original, all in Sweden and Finland.

The lion's share of today's frontier forest – more than 75 percent – is located in just three large tracts covering parts of seven countries: two blocks of boreal forest – one stretching across much of Canada and Alaska and the other in Russia – and one large relatively undisturbed chunk of tropical forest spanning the Northwestern Amazon Basin and Guyana Shield.

FIGURE 3

Temperate Frontier Forests Are the Most Endangered...

PERCENT OF THE WORLD'S FRONTIER FORESTS

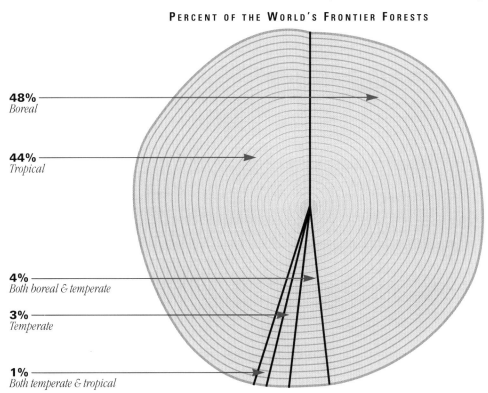

48%
Boreal

44%
Tropical

4%
Both boreal & temperate

3%
Temperate

1%
Both temperate & tropical

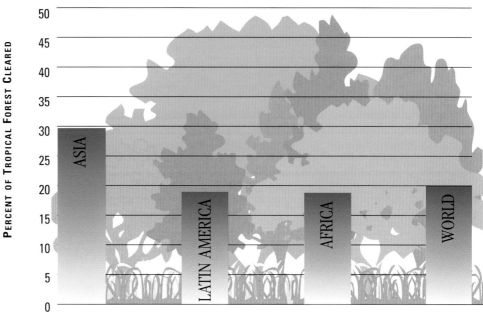

Percentage of the World's Tropical Forest Cleared Between 1960 and 1990

PERCENT OF TROPICAL FOREST CLEARED

50
45
40
35
30
25
20
15
10
5
0

ASIA

LATIN AMERICA

AFRICA

WORLD

Source: Singh and Marzoli, 1995

2

FRONTIER FOREST MYTHS

As places that conjure up images of vast, empty spaces, frontiers are associated with many popular myths that contribute to their destruction. In each case, the reality is far more complex. Three of the more common myths about frontier forests are:

MYTH: Frontiers are comprised of empty wilderness.

REALITY: People have lived in many forests for hundreds of generations, mostly in small groups. Forests today house several hundred million people in Asia alone,[25] while at least 20 million people live in the Amazon Basin.[26] Low-level human activity over thousands of years within these areas has helped shape the forest structure and species mix in frontier ecosystems.

MYTH: Forest peoples live in utopian harmony with nature.

REALITY: Long before European colonization, forest peoples managed their natural resources according to customary practices. Evidence suggests that some human cultures destroyed their own forest ecosystems through abuse, and others in tribal warfare.[27,28] Today, rising populations, land shortages, and access to sophisticated technologies pose further management challenges for forest peoples.

MYTH: Frontiers consist of fertile land, ripe for development.

REALITY: In many places, frontier forests remain undeveloped because their soils are poor and they don't have much commercially valuable timber per hectare. In many tropical forests, for instance, intensive agricultural activity can rapidly deplete soils that need natural debris from the tree canopy. Then too, forests are finite, and some are inaccessible. Forests in Amazonia and in Central Africa, for example, are rich in biodiversity but they often lack high densities of valuable timber species or good soils.[29]

WORLD RESOURCES INSTITUTE   **14**   FOREST FRONTIERS INITIATIVE

Many of the frontier forests that have survived into this century may not make it into the next. Results from this study suggest that 39 percent of the world's remaining frontiers are threatened – that is, under moderate or high threat – by logging, agricultural clearing, and other activities, often along the forest edges. Many frontier forests not yet threatened – particularly those in the tropics – are still vulnerable because they contain valuable timber, oil, or minerals.

Most of the safest frontier forests are in the far north, where resource-extraction costs are high. Taking these forests out of the global calculus changes it significantly: outside Russia and Canada, three quarters of the world's frontier forests – including virtually all temperate forest frontiers – are at risk.

The most important threats to frontier forests are described below:

■ **LOGGING**: This study suggests that commercial logging poses by far the greatest danger to frontier forests. In all six regions assessed, WRI's advisors cited logging as the predominate threat to forests – affecting more than 70 percent of the world's threatened frontiers. *(See Table 2.)* Logging can significantly "rewrite" the structure and composition of forests. Yet, some of its most negative effects are indirect:

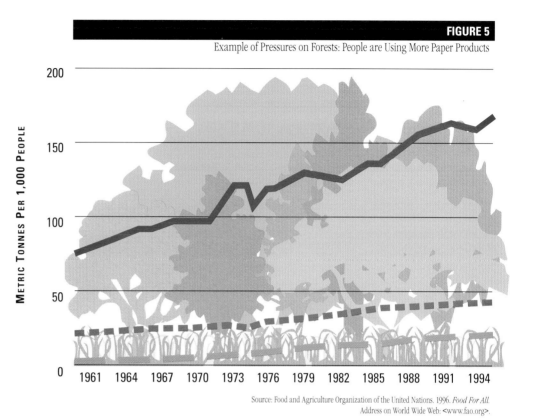

FIGURE 5

Example of Pressures on Forests: People are Using More Paper Products

Source: Food and Agriculture Organization of the United Nations. 1996. *Food For All.*
Address on World Wide Web: <www.fao.org>.

INDUSTRIALIZED COUNTRIES   WORLD   DEVELOPING COUNTRIES

logging offsets the cost of road-building to extract the timber, which in turn opens forests to hunting, fuelwood gathering, and clearing for agriculture. Widely considered the primary cause of tropical deforestation (when frontier and non-frontier forest are taken together), agricultural clearing, in particular, is hastened once loggers open forests up.[30,31]

■ **ENERGY DEVELOPMENT, MINING, AND NEW INFRASTRUCTURE**: Large-scale mining and exploration for petroleum and natural gas also bring new roads and settlements that open once-inaccessible forests to other human activities. Damming rivers for hydroelectric power floods millions of hectares of

forest and disrupts freshwater ecosystems. These operations also take up forest land and spew pollution into the environment. Energy development, mining, and the roads, pipelines, and settlements that come with it represent the second biggest threat to frontier forests globally, affecting close to 40 percent of all frontiers classified as under moderate or high threat.

LAND CLEARING FOR AGRICULTURE: One fifth of the world's threatened frontiers are directly endangered by farmers who clear forest for cropland and pasture. Land clearing is particularly rapacious in Asia, Africa, and Latin America. This threat can only grow as population increases. For the record, results from WRI's study suggest that non-frontier forests – often crisscrossed by roads and easily accessible – are under much greater pressure from farmers than are frontier forests.

EXCESSIVE VEGETATION REMOVAL: Apart from logging and outright clearing, humans are removing millions of tons of vegetation from frontier forests, pulling at the fabric of these ecosystems. WRI found that about 14 percent of the world's threatened frontiers are being degraded by overgrazing or the overcollection of firewood, building materials, and other vegetation. Besides damaging terrestrial habitats, excessive vegetation removal causes the rivers and streams that run through these forests to silt up.

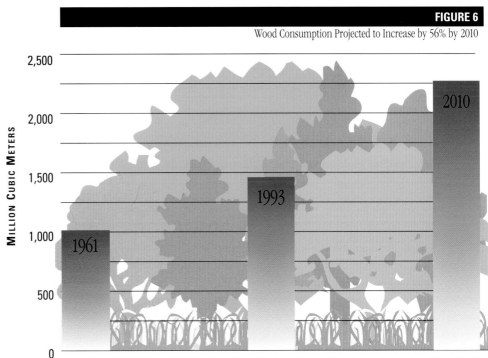

FIGURE 6

Wood Consumption Projected to Increase by 56% by 2010

Source: Food and Agriculture Organization of the United Nations. 1996. *Food For All.*
Address on World Wide Web: <www.fao.org>.

OVERHUNTING: As ecosystems, frontier forests comprise more than just trees. Local extinctions of animal species can affect the integrity of the entire forest. Many species – including elephants in Africa and beaver in North America – distribute tree seeds and otherwise shape forest structure. In Africa, one third of the forest frontier which is threatened is at risk through commercial hunting, driven largely by urban demand for bushmeat.

OTHER THREATS: On a smaller scale, other activities also endanger frontier forests. They range from the obvious – forest conversion to, say, tree plantations or ski resorts – to the not so obvious. Among the latter are forest managers who suppress natural fires which help shape many frontier ecosystems, far-off factories that emit wind-borne pollutants harmful to trees, and exotic animal species introduced either accidentally or deliberately by people who don't know or don't care that the newcomers can outcompete native plants and animals for scarce resources. (In New Zealand, our advisors concluded that introduced and feral species – domestic species gone wild – pose the single greatest danger to frontier forests.)

In most cases, frontier forests are endangered by more than one of these threats. One future threat not covered in this study is the potential impact of global warming on forest ecosystems. Native species that can't adapt or migrate to new habitats quickly enough could die out rapidly as climate changes and new diseases, pest infestations, and natural disturbances increase as a result.[32]

DESTRUCTION'S ROOTS

Frequently, governments and industry reap the profits while frontier peoples receive only a sliver of the benefits but bear the environmental brunt of forest mismanagement.

Like symptoms of disease, visible threats to forests are often best treated by addressing their underlying causes. Behind the obvious activities endangering the world's frontier forests are a nest of interrelated root causes:

■ **GROWING ECONOMIES AND CONSUMPTION**: Even in parts of the world where population is not growing significantly, demand for certain forest resources – for both local and export markets – is intensifying as economies expand. Between 1961 and 1994, per capita consumption of paper increased by 86 percent globally and by 350 percent in developing countries. *(See Figure 5.)* Industrialized countries still use more than 10 times as much paper per person than people in developing regions do. Global consumption of industrial wood products is expected to jump by more than 50 percent by 2010. *(See Figure 6.)*

■ **POPULATION GROWTH AND DEMAND FOR NEW LAND**: Just since 1950, the world's population has more than doubled.[33] As a result, in many regions, forests have been cleared to grow food and to make way for new settlements. Population growth also drives up demand for timber, paper, fuelwood, and other products from an ever-shrinking forest base.

TABLE 2

Threats to Frontier Forests

		PERCENT OF THREATENED FOREST FRONTIERS AT RISK FROM:				
REGION	PERCENT OF FRONTIER FOREST UNDER MODERATE OR HIGH THREAT (i)	LOGGING	MINING, ROADS AND OTHER INFRASTRUCTURE	AGRICULTURAL CLEARING	EXCESSIVE VEGETATION REMOVAL	OTHER (ii)
Africa	77	79	12	17	8	41
Asia	60	50	10	20	9	24
North & Central America	29	83	27	3	1	14
Central America	87	54	17	23	29	13
North America	26	84	27	2	0	14
South America	54	69	53	32	14	5
Russia & Europe	19	86	51	4	29	18
Europe	100	80	0	0	20	0
Russia	19	86	51	4	29	18
Oceania (iii)	76	42	25	15	38	27
World	39	72	38	20	14	13

Notes: (i) Frontier forests considered under immediate threat, as a percent of all frontier forest assessed for threat. Threatened frontier forests are places where ongoing or planned human activities are likely, if continued over coming decades, to result in the significant loss of natural qualities associated with all or part of these areas (for example, causing declines in, or local extinctions of, wildlife and plant populations, or large-scale changes in the age and structure of these forests).

(ii) "Other" includes such activities as overhunting, introduction of harmful exotic species, isolation of smaller frontier forest 'islands' through development of surrounding lands, changes in fire regimes and plantation establishment.

(iii) Oceania consists of Papua New Guinea, Australia and New Zealand.

See Technical Annex.

■ **BAD ECONOMIC POLICIES**:
In weighing land-management options, economists and policy-makers often overlook the costs of losing frontier forest. Such costs may come in the form of soil erosion, the loss of water for agriculture, and release of carbon into the atmosphere. Lost opportunities should count too, including foregone income from ecotourism, "bio-prospecting", and other lucrative uses of whole and healthy forests. Even logging, mining and other exploitative uses often don't bring in the revenues they could: trying to attract foreign investors, many national governments all but give away valuable rights to exploit their forests. Such economic decisions are common because the costs of destruction are not felt or paid by those doing the damage. Frequently, governments and industry reap the profits while frontier peoples receive only a sliver of the benefits but bear the environmental brunt of forest mismanagement.

---

3 | **DIFFERENT WAYS OF RANKING COUNTRIES**

WRI's Forest Frontiers Index speaks volumes about the countries' opportunities to protect frontier forests and about the immediacy of threats to these frontiers. Alternative methods for ranking countries tell different stories. Table 4, for example, identifies the 12 countries with the largest area of frontier forest. All told, these countries account for 90 percent of what remains on Earth. Table 5 lists countries with frontier forest likely to be of exceptional biodiversity value (based on the large numbers of plant species estimated to be found within them).

One important story – beyond the scope of this assessment – would be to rank countries according to the amount of threatened forest lying outside frontiers. Such an index would be useful for identifying countries where unique forest ecosystems are on the verge of extinction.

■ **SHORT-SIGHTED POLITICAL DECISIONS**: In much of the world, frontier forests are sacrificed for short-term political gain – to appease interest groups or to line the pockets of politicians and their allies. In endangered U.S. and Canadian old-growth forests, for example, governments allow logging to provide questionable job security for a very small number of people who may soon be sidelined by technological and market changes within the industry anyway. In tropical countries such as Brazil, Indonesia, and Malaysia, decision makers attack poverty by moving millions of people to the forest frontier, even though this approach is only a temporary fix for the poor and can permanently destroy the forests.

■ **CORRUPTION AND ILLEGAL TRADE**: Corruption among officials in government, industry, and other organizations often hastens frontier forest loss. In Cambodia, for example, the military takes part in a thriving illegal timber trade with neighboring Thailand.[34] In Burma, the government and rebel groups have both financed a decades-long civil war with illegal logging proceeds.[35] In Alaska, Malaysia, Suriname, and elsewhere, timber companies have been accused of engaging in timber smuggling, trying to bribe government officials to procure lucrative concessions, and other illegal practices.[36,37] Even demand for illegal drugs fuels forest destruction: in Colombia, for example, clearings are carved out of remote frontier forests to grow coca, marijuana, and opium poppies. [38]

■ **POVERTY AND LANDLESSNESS**: In Brazil, Guatemala, and elsewhere, the poor flock to frontier forests in search of agricultural land and other economic opportunities. Rather than grapple with such politically thorny issues as land redistribution and tenure, governments often encourage the clearing of forest lands poorly suited to agriculture. In Brazil, for example, migrants have had to clear forest to establish land ownership, a "don't think twice" policy that spawned more deforestation and discouraged settlers from managing frontiers for their forest products. [39]

THE FRONTIER FOREST INDEX

WRI's Frontier Forest Index shows that most of the world's nations have already lost, or might soon lose, their last frontier forests. *(See Table 3.)* The index ranks countries according to the percentage of frontier forest lost and to the proportion of remaining frontier that is moderately or highly threatened – in other words, high-scoring countries have lost much of their frontier, and most of what remains is threatened.

Seventy-six countries have lost it all. These include almost all of the countries of Europe and Eastern Africa and all of North Africa and the Middle East. For these countries, forest restoration should be a priority. *(See Box 4.)*

Another 11 countries – including Nigeria, Thailand, Sweden, Finland and Guatemala – are classified as on the edge. They have at most 5 percent of their original frontier left, and it is threatened. While core areas of these isolated frontiers may be protected in parks or reserves, logging and other activities outside (and sometimes inside) protected areas threaten the ecosystems as a whole. Unless these countries act immediately, they are likely to lose most of the little frontier they have left.

In 28 countries, there is not much time to protect remaining frontier forests. Most of these nations have lost most of their original frontier, and much of the remainder is threatened. These countries include the United States (which, if not for Alaska's vast boreal forest, would rank among countries "on the edge"), Papua New Guinea, Malaysia, Panama, Mexico, Argentina, India, and Australia.

Only seven countries – Brazil, Suriname, Guyana, Canada, Colombia, Venezuela, and Russia – and one Overseas Department of France (French Guiana), still have a large proportion of their original forest cover remaining in an unthreatened state. These nations have great opportunities to sustain large areas of frontier forest if they begin to follow stewardship principles now. *(See Box 5.)*

Even in these eight places, some frontiers are under siege. In Canada, two thirds of British Columbia's temperate coastal rainforest – one of Earth's biologically richest temperate ecosystems – has been degraded by logging or other development, and much of what remains intact outside protected areas is slated for logging in coming years. [40] International timber companies have been trying to negotiate contracts to log much of the remaining Amazon and Guyana Shield frontier – including one third of Suriname's forests. [41] Decisions made within the next few years will decide the fate of frontier forests within these countries.

TABLE 3

Frontier Forest Index

COUNTRY	PERCENT OF ORIGINAL FRONTIER FOREST LOST	PERCENT OF CURRENT FRONTIER FOREST THREATENED	FRONTIER FOREST INDEX (99 = WORST POSSIBLE SCORE)

LOST IT ALL *(These countries have lost all of their frontier forest. Restoration should be a priority.)*

Afghanistan, Albania, Algeria, Angola, Armenia, Austria, Azerbaijan, Belgium, Benin, Botswana, Bulgaria, Burundi, Byelarus, Czech Republic, Denmark, El Salvador, Equatorial Guinea, Eritrea, Estonia, Ethiopia, France, The Gambia, Georgia, Germany, Ghana, Greece, Guinea, Guinea-Bissau, Hungary, Iran, Ireland, Italy, Japan, Kenya, Democratic People's Republic of Korea, Republic of Korea, Kyrgyzstan, Latvia, Lebanon, Liberia, Lithuania, Luxembourg, Madagascar, Moldova, Morocco, Mozambique, Namibia, Nepal, Netherlands, Pakistan, Paraguay, Philippines, Poland, Portugal, Romania, Rwanda, Sao Tome and Principe, Senegal, Sierra Leone, Slovakia, South Africa, Spain, Switzerland, Tajikistan, Tanzania, Togo, Tunisia, Turkey, Turkmenistan, Uganda, Ukraine, United Kingdom, Uzbekistan, Yugoslavia (former), Zambia, Zimbabwe.

ON THE EDGE *(Unless they act immediately, these countries risk losing much of their remaining frontier forest)*

Country	% Lost	% Threatened	Index
Nigeria	99	100	99
Finland	99	100	99
Vietnam	98	100	98
Laos	98	100	98
Guatemala	98	100	98
Cote d'Ivoire	98	100	98
Taiwan	98	100	98
Sweden	97	100	97
Bangladesh	96	100	96
Central African Republic	96	100	96
Thailand	95	100	95

NOT MUCH TIME *(Frontier forest in these countries will continue to fall without further action.)*

Country	% Lost	% Threatened	Index
Argentina	94	100	94
New Zealand	91	100	91
China	98	93	91
Costa Rica	90	100	90
Cambodia	90	100	90
Cameroon	92	97	90
Brunei	89	100	89
Honduras	84	100	84
United States	94	85	79
Nicaragua	78	100	78
Bhutan	76	100	76
Mexico	92	77	71
Gabon	68	100	68
Sri Lanka	88	76	67
Panama	65	100	65
Ecuador	63	99	63
Zaire	84	70	59
India	99	57	56
Bolivia	56	97	55
Burma	94	56	52
Australia	82	63	52
Papua New Guinea	60	84	50
Congo	71	65	46
Belize	65	66	43
Malaysia	85	48	41
Peru	43	95	41
Indonesia	72	54	39
Chile	45	76	35

GREAT OPPORTUNITY *(Given careful stewardship, these countries have a real chance to keep most of their original frontier forest.)*

Country	% Lost	% Threatened	Index
Brazil	58	48	28
Venezuela	41	37	15
Russia	71	19	13
Colombia	64	19	12
Canada	42	21	8
Guyana	18	41	7
Suriname	8	22	2
French Guiana	8	0	0

TABLE 4

Countries With Most of the World's Remaining Frontier Forest

GLOBAL RANK	COUNTRY	TOTAL FRONTIER FOREST (000 KM²)	PERCENT OF THE WORLD'S TOTAL FRONTIER FOREST
1	Russia	3,448	26
2	Canada	3,429	25
3	Brazil	2,284	17
4	Peru	540	4
5	Indonesia	530	4
6	Venezuela	391	3
7	Colombia	348	3
8	United States	307	2
9	Zaire	292	2
10	Bolivia	255	2
11	Papua New Guinea	172	1
12	Chile	162	1

Total frontier forest area of the top 12 countries as a % of the global total: 90

TABLE 5

Ten Countries with the Highest Plant Biodiversity in Their Frontier Forest

GLOBAL RANK	COUNTRY	FRONTIER FOREST (000 KM²)	ESTIMATED NUMBER OF PLANT SPECIES WITHIN FRONTIER FORESTS (THOUSANDS)	PERCENT OF THE COUNTRY'S PLANT SPECIES FOUND WITHIN FRONTIER FORESTS
1	Brazil	2,284	36	~65
2	Colombia	348	34	~70
3	Indonesia	530	18	~65
4	Venezuela	391	15	~75
5	Peru	540	13	~75
6	Ecuador	80	12	~65
7	Bolivia	255	10	~60
8	Mexico	87	9	~35
9	Malaysia	47	8	~50
10	Papua New Guinea	172	7	~70

Note: Forest frontier plant species richness was estimated by multiplying the country's higher plant species totals per unit area (standardized for size, using a species-area curve) by the country's total frontier forest area.

NORTH AND CENTRAL AMERICA

After Russia's, the world's largest expanse of frontier forest is an unbroken 6,500-kilometer arc of boreal forest stretching from Newfoundland to Alaska. These North American forest ecosystems – still vast and relatively undisturbed in northernmost Canada and interior Alaska – store a significant proportion of the global total of biotic carbon and supply much of the world's growing demand for forest products. They also provide livelihoods for thousands of indigenous people and a refuge for woodland caribou, grizzly bear, grey wolf, and other large mammals that once ranged widely across the continent. [42] As a group, these frontiers rank among the least threatened in the world (approximately a quarter of the area is threatened). Even so, they are being pushed steadily northward by mineral extraction, hydroelectric development, and skyrocketing demand for wood fiber, especially paper products.

To the south, North America's temperate frontier forests have retreated to a few remote mountainous pockets in the western United States and Canada. Within the lower 48 U.S. states, frontiers account for about 1 percent of original forest cover.

North American forest ecosystems store a significant proportion of the global total of biotic carbon and supply much of the world's growing demand for forest products.

What remains lies primarily within three assemblages of national parks and wilderness areas in the northern Rockies and one block in the North Cascades of Washington state. While each forest block is largely protected, they are classified as threatened because they are becoming too isolated to support populations of some of their large mammal species over time. [43]

In Mexico, one relatively large frontier remains in the Sierra Madre Occidental, a biologically diverse temperate conifer forest severely threatened by rapidly expanding logging and road construction. Mexico's other frontier forests are in Oaxaca, Chiapas, and the Maya forest region (which extends into Belize and Guatemala). These tropical forests – along with a chain of others stretching south through the Miskito coast of Honduras and Nicaragua, the La Amistad region on the Costa Rican-Panamanian border, and the Darien forests on Panama's border with Colombia – are almost all highly threatened.

Central America's frontier forests are under many kinds of assault. In the Darien region, the major threat is completion of the Pan American highway. *(See below.)* In other areas, agricultural expansion, logging, and infrastructure development are the dangers. Guatemala's forest frontier, for example, shrank dramatically in the past decade as logging roads opened the area to landless peasants and to wealthy agricultural business interests.

On the whole, North America still has a good number of frontier forests in its northernmost regions that remain relatively safe. Yet from its southern band of boreal forests all the way to Panama's Darien Gap, virtually all the rest of the continent's frontiers stand to lose their frontier status within the next decade or two.

Frontier:
1. TONGAS NATIONAL FOREST
Forest type: Temperate
Geographic location: Alaska, United States
Threat: Logging
At risk: One of the world's largest tracts of temperate old-growth forest, as well as a unique ecosystem type: coastal temperate rainforest.

Frontier:
2. FORESTS OF THE DARIEN GAP
Forest type: Tropical
Geographic location: Panama and Colombia
Threat: Logging, other wood removal, proposed highway construction, and coca cultivation
At risk: A proposed highway across the Darien Gap would provide a route for non-indigenous species – such as organisms that cause hoof-and-mouth disease – with potentially disastrous long-term biological and economic consequences to both regions. [44,45] Road construction, logging, and other activities threaten forests that are home to three indigenous cultures and rich native biodiversity.

THREATENED FRONTIER FORESTS OF NORTH AMERICA

FRONTIER FORESTS UNDER LOW OR NO THREAT: large, intact natural forest ecosystems that are relatively undisturbed and large enough to maintain all of their biodiversity.

FRONTIER FORESTS UNDER MEDIUM OR HIGH THREAT: ongoing or planned human activities (e.g. logging, agricultural clearing, mining) will, if continued, significantly degrade these frontiers.

NON-FRONTIER FORESTS: secondary forest, plantations, degraded forest, and patches of primary forest not meeting this study's criteria as frontier.

FRONTIER FORESTS UNASSESSED FOR THREAT: insufficient information prevented evaluating the threat level of these frontiers.

Map Projection: Lambert-Azimuthal. Basemap data from ArcWorld. Assistance in data preparation, mapping, and analysis provided by *World Wildlife Fund &* World Conservation Monitoring Centre. *Data sources (i.) Forest cover data provided by World Conservation Monitoring Centre. (ii.) Frontier forest data derived through expert assessment and from other sources.*

WORLD RESOURCES INSTITUTE   FOREST FRONTIERS INITIATIVE

THREATENED FRONTIER FORESTS OF SOUTH AMERICA

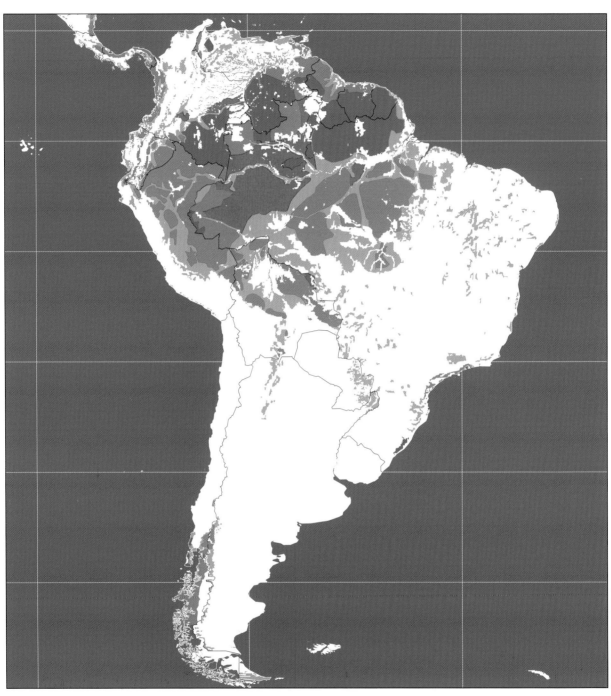

FRONTIER FORESTS UNDER LOW OR NO THREAT:
large, intact natural forest ecosystems that are relatively undisturbed and large enough to maintain all of their biodiversity.

FRONTIER FORESTS UNDER MEDIUM OR HIGH THREAT:
ongoing or planned human activities (e.g. logging, agricultural clearing, mining) will, if continued, significantly degrade these frontiers.

NON-FRONTIER FORESTS:
secondary forest, plantations, degraded forest, and patches of primary forest not meeting this study's criteria as frontier.

FRONTIER FORESTS UNASSESSED FOR THREAT:
insufficient information prevented evaluating the threat level of these frontiers.

Basemap data from ArcWorld. Assistance in data preparation, mapping and analysis provided by 🐼 *World Wildlife Fund &* *World Conservation Monitoring Centre.*
Data sources (i.) Forest cover data provided by World Conservation Monitoring Centre. (ii.) Forest frontiers data derived through expert assessment and from other sources.

WORLD RESOURCES INSTITUTE　　FOREST FRONTIERS INITIATIVE

Logging is the main threat to South America's frontier forests.

SOUTH AMERICA

Throughout South America, large-scale resettlement and agricultural and resource development projects claimed much of the 645,000 square kilometers of forest lost in this region between 1980 and 1990 – the greatest amount of forest loss in the world during these years. Brazil alone lost close to 370,000 square kilometers – more than a fifth of all tropical forest lost worldwide during that time. [46]

Still, South America maintains vast areas of intact tropical and temperate forest. The Northern Amazon Basin and the Guyana Shield house the largest tropical frontier forests anywhere. [47]

On the rim of the Amazon Basin, forests of the Northern Andes (Peru, Ecuador, and Colombia) rank among Earth's biologically richest. [48] Chile and Argentina share the largest single block of remaining temperate frontier forest in the world.

Logging is the main threat to South America's frontier forests, endangering about 70 percent of all frontiers classified under medium or high threat. Energy exploration, mining, and new roads are encroaching on about half the region's threatened frontiers. Clearing for agriculture jeopardizes almost a third of all threatened frontier forests.

In recent decades, national development policies have fueled much of the region's deforestation. During the 1960s and 1970s, the Brazilian government's "modernization" policy prompted major forest clearing in the Amazon. The government had hoped to solve land-tenure problems in other regions by establishing colonies of small-holder farmers in the forests, to integrate the region into the rest of the country with a massive road network, earn revenues by developing natural resources and strengthen Brazil's borders by populating its frontier. Government policies triggered both planned and spontaneous immigration of landless peasants from throughout the country, and resulted in large-scale clearing of the forest by land speculators hoping to profit from subsidies provided to cattle ranchers. [49,50]

In Bolivia, Guyana, and Suriname, a drive to exploit natural resources over the past decade – partly to respond to economic crises – has accelerated the loss of frontier forests. Only Venezuela and Colombia have strongly restricted logging, mining, and other extractive activities, and Venezuela may soon buckle under severe economic pressure to exploit its rich natural resources.

Chile's temperate frontier forests are increasingly threatened, primarily by logging to provide wood chips (for export mainly to Japan) and fuelwood. While Eucalyptus and pine plantations provide much of the timber needed for export and industry, precious native forests are cleared to make way for new plantations. [51,52]

THREATENED FRONTIERS INCLUDE:

Frontier:
1. THE ATLANTIC RAINFOREST
Forest type: Tropical
Geographic location: Coastal Brazil
Threats: Logging, agricultural clearing, excessive vegetation removal, pollution
At Risk: Only 5 percent of the original Atlantic Rainforest is left, and just a fraction of this vestige can be considered frontier. The Atlantic Rainforest is particularly rich in biodiversity: 70 percent of its plants and most of its 20 primate species are found nowhere else in the world, and the wild relatives of many important food crops (including pineapple, cassava, sweet potato, and papaya) are found there.

Frontier:
2. COASTAL CHILEAN FORESTS
Forest type: Temperate
Geographic location: Southern Chile
Threats: Clearing for plantations, logging for the wood-chip industry, fuelwood production
At Risk: One third of the world's largest tract of relatively undisturbed temperate forest. Chile's temperate forests contain at least 50 species of timber trees (95 percent of them endemic) and more than 700 vascular plant species (half of them endemic). [53] The alerce cedar, the Southern Hemisphere's largest conifer and a tree that can live over 3,000 years, is found here. [54] More than 35,000 families in this region face severe poverty and expulsion as large timber companies buy land for wood-chip production and tree plantations.

Frontier:
3. BOLÍVAR STATE
Forest type: Tropical
Geographic location: Southeastern Venezuela
Threats: Logging, mining (gold and diamonds), and oil exploration.
At Risk: Venezuela's Bolívar State is a part of the Guyana Shield-Amazon Basin complex, the largest tropical frontier forest. Rich in species, the area is home to the Pemón and several other indigenous groups.

Only Brazil, Suriname, Guyana, Canada, Colombia, Venezuela, Russia, and French Guiana still have a large proportion of their original forest cover remaining in an unthreatened state.

AFRICA

Except for the Congo Basin, Africa's frontier forests have largely been destroyed, primarily by loggers and by farmers clearing land for agriculture. In West Africa, nearly 90 percent of the original moist forest is gone, and what remains is heavily fragmented and degraded. Today, West African frontiers are restricted to one patch in Cote d'Ivoire and another along the border between Nigeria and Cameroon.

To the east, very little remains of Madagascar's once magnificent tropical forests. Long isolated from mainland ecosystems, these forests are home to an exceptional number of plants and animals found nowhere else. Unfortunately, none of Madagascar's forest fragments is large or natural enough to qualify as a frontier today.

Large blocks of intact natural forest do remain in Central Africa, particularly in Zaire, Gabon, and the Congo. In Zaire – which contains more than half this region's forest cover – many forests remain intact, in part because the nation's poor transportation system can't easily handle timber and mineral exploitation.[55] Some areas have fewer passable roads today than in 1960, the year the country became independent, and some frontiers have lost population during this period.

Today, most of Africa's remaining frontier forests are at risk. The two major threats are logging and commercial hunting to meet growing urban demand for bushmeat. (Overhunting removes populations of key species that help maintain natural forest ecosystems.) In Central Africa, over 90 percent of all logging occurs in primary forest – one of the highest ratios of any region in the world.[56] In some areas, logging itself causes relatively little damage because only a few high-value tree species are removed. Still, logging roads open up a forest to hunters, would-be farmers and other profit-seekers. One region warranting special concern is eastern Zaire: Civil unrest in Rwanda, Burundi, Sudan, and Zaire has driven hundreds of thousands of people into this area, where they escalate demands on the forest.

THREATENED FRONTIERS INCLUDE:

Frontier:
1. TAI NATIONAL PARK AND SURROUNDING FORESTS
Forest type: Tropical
Geographic location: Cote d'Ivoire
Threats: Logging, agricultural clearing, hunting, potential invasion by war refugees
At Risk: The only remaining large and relatively intact piece of a forest block that once covered more than 830,000 square kilometers in eight countries west of the Dahomey Gap (a natural savanna that divides West Africa's forests into two distinct sections).

Frontier:
2. CROSS RIVER AND KORUP NATIONAL PARKS AND SURROUNDING FORESTS
Forest type: Tropical
Geographic location: Border between Nigeria and Cameroon
Threats: Logging by Asian and European timber companies in unprotected forests, new settlements, agricultural clearing, hunting
At risk: Rich in plant species, this forest may provide a wealth of potential new drugs and industrial products. Extracts from the newly discovered Ancistrocladus korupensis vine, for example, offer hope for a new AIDS treatment.

Except for the Congo Basin, Africa's frontier forests have largely been destroyed, and most of those remaining are at risk.

Frontier:
3. EASTERN ZAIRE FORESTS
Forest type: Tropical
Geographic location: Zaire
Threats: Agricultural clearing, invasion by throngs of war refugees
At risk: The greatest biological diversity of any forests on the continent. Also, the Ituri forest (found within this frontier) is home to many of Africa's remaining pygmy peoples.

THREATENED FRONTIER FORESTS OF AFRICA

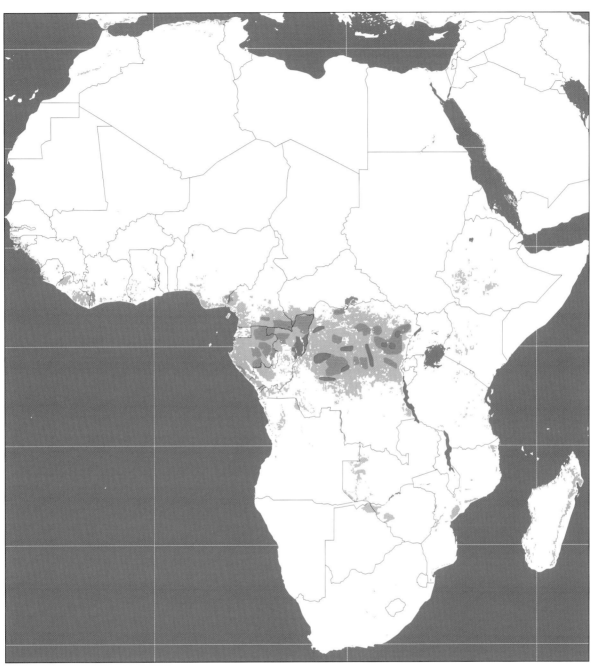

FRONTIER FORESTS UNDER LOW OR NO THREAT: large, intact natural forest ecosystems that are relatively undisturbed and large enough to maintain all of their biodiversity.

FRONTIER FORESTS UNDER MEDIUM OR HIGH THREAT: ongoing or planned human activities (e.g. logging, agricultural clearing, mining) will, if continued, significantly degrade these frontiers.

NON-FRONTIER FORESTS: secondary forest, plantations, degraded forest, and patches of primary forest not meeting this study's criteria as frontier.

FRONTIER FORESTS UNASSESSED FOR THREAT: insufficient information prevented evaluating the threat level of these frontiers.

Basemap data from ArcWorld. Assistance in data preparation, mapping and analysis provided by 🐼 *World Wildlife Fund &* 🌐 *World Conservation Monitoring Centre. Data sources (i.) Forest cover data provided by World Conservation Monitoring Centre. (ii.) Forest frontiers data derived through expert assessment and from other sources.*

WORLD RESOURCES INSTITUTE   FOREST FRONTIERS INITIATIVE

THREATENED FRONTIER FORESTS OF EUROPE & RUSSIA

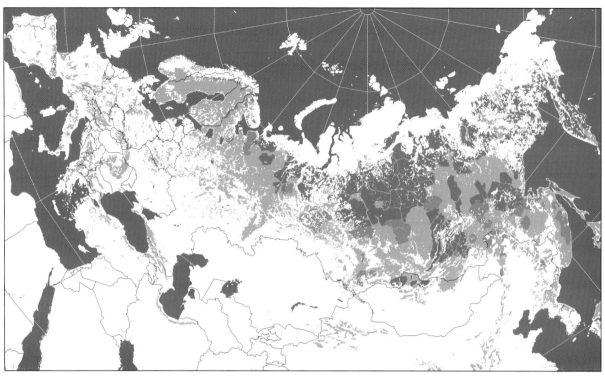

■ **FRONTIER FORESTS UNDER LOW OR NO THREAT:** large, intact natural forest ecosystems that are relatively undisturbed and large enough to maintain all of their biodiversity.	■ **FRONTIER FORESTS UNDER MEDIUM OR HIGH THREAT:** ongoing or planned human activities (e.g. logging, agricultural clearing, mining) will, if continued, significantly degrade these frontiers.	■ **NON-FRONTIER FORESTS:** secondary forest, plantations, degraded forest, and patches of primary forest not meeting this study's criteria as frontier.	■ **FRONTIER FORESTS UNASSESSED FOR THREAT:** insufficient information prevented evaluating the threat level of these frontiers.

Map Projection: Equidistant. Basemap data from ArcWorld. Assistance in data preparation, mapping and analysis provided by ★ World Wildlife Fund & ▦ World Conservation Monitoring Centre. Data sources (i.) Forest cover data provided by World Conservation Monitoring Centre. (ii.) Forest frontiers data derived through expert assessment and from other sources.

EUROPE AND RUSSIA

Once blanketed by forest, Europe and Russia have both lost virtually all of their temperate frontier forest. Most of Europe's forests were leveled centuries ago. Although forest area within the region has increased since 1950, nearly all of it consists of plantation or highly managed forest.[57]

Europe's last few large tracts of relatively natural forest are in Sweden and Finland. Significant portions of this frontier fall outside parks and reserves, and all frontier forests are threatened by road development, fire suppression, grazing, logging, and other activities.

Containing Earth's largest expanse of frontier forest (mostly in Siberia), Russia's boreal forests are still largely intact. The country houses almost three quarters of all boreal forest and nearly one fifth of the world's total forest area.[58] An immense storehouse of living carbon, the nation's frontier forests cover more than 4 million square kilometers. Clearing them could contribute significantly to global warming. Russia's Far Eastern frontier is also the last habitat for such highly endangered species as the Amur tiger, the Far Eastern leopard, the Far Eastern forest cat, the red wolf, and the sikha deer.[59]

Endangered frontier forests in Russia are threatened mainly by logging, named by WRI's advisors as the chief risk in about 85 percent of the region's threatened frontier forest. Mineral and energy exploration and set fires also impinge.

Already, portions of Russia's Far East and much of European Russia (west of the Ural mountains) have been heavily logged. Until now, lack of infrastructure and outmoded harvesting practices kept much of Siberia's frontier forest undeveloped. Recent economic and political liberalization may change the situation, however. International timber and trading corporations, particularly Asian companies, are looking to Siberian forests as a new source of supply as burgeoning global demand for timber strips other regions of valuable, accessible trees.[60] Over the next decade or two, foreign capital, machinery, and road-building could open much of Siberia's forest to logging, mining, and other damaging activities.

Frontier:
1. NORTHERN PRIMORSKI KRAI
Forest type: Temperate and boreal
Geographic location: Russian Far East
Threats: Logging, mining, and road development
At risk: Habitat for some of the world's rarest species, including the Amur tiger. This forest also is home to Udege, Nanai, Ul'ta, and other indigenous groups.[61]

Frontier:
2. FRONTIERS ENCOMPASSING THE GREEN KARELIAN BELT
Forest type: Boreal
Geographic location: Russia and Finland
Threats: Logging for export to Finland and related road construction
At risk: One of Europe's last remaining frontiers and the traditional home of the Karelian people.

ASIA

Asia has lost almost 95 percent of its frontier forests. Apart from the Mediterranean and Middle East – where all such forests have disappeared – this represents the world's greatest loss of frontier forest outside of Europe. China and India today have just 20 percent of their original forest cover. Of these remaining forests, less than 10 percent can be classified as frontier. In the 20 years between 1960 and 1980 alone, Asia lost almost a third of its tropical forest cover, the highest rate of forest conversion in the world.[62]

On mainland Southeast Asia, most frontiers are gone. The isolated pockets left are confined primarily to Burma, Laos, and Cambodia, where war and civil unrest until recently inhibited development. With peace have come new threats from commercial loggers who have already exhausted forests in Thailand and peninsular Malaysia – where harvest and import restrictions now encourage logging companies to move on to neighboring nations.

Most of Asia's remaining frontier forest is confined to the islands of Borneo, Sumatra, Sulawesi, and Irian Jaya. Even here, however, loggers have exploited most accessible forests along coasts and major rivers. Agriculture and poorly planned resettlement programs also take a toll. Between 1969 and 1994, Indonesia's transmigration program moved 8 million people to the nation's forested islands where 1.7 million hectares of tropical forest were soon stripped.[63]

More than half of Asia's last frontiers are under moderate to high threat, particularly from logging. An even greater long-term worry is Asia's burgeoning population and its ever increasing demand for food and agricultural land. Between 1990 and 1995 alone, the region's largely rural population grew by more than 270 million people. The world's most densely populated region, Asia had more than 1 person for every hectare of land in 1995.[64]

THREATENED FRONTIERS INCLUDE:

Frontier:
1. RATANAKIRI PROVINCE
Forest type: Tropical
Geographic location: Cambodia
Threat: Illegal logging for export to Vietnam. Outside protected areas, most of the province is already under concession to foreign logging companies.
At risk: Resident minority groups, already evicted from other areas by logging companies. Rice farming and local fishing here and elsewhere in the Mekong River watershed. Kouprey and other highly endangered species.

Frontier:
2. SUNDARBANS
Forest type: Tropical
Geographic location: Bangladesh and India
Threat: Logging, fuelwood collection
At risk: The world's largest mangrove forest. Habitat for the world's largest – and possibly only viable – population of the Bengal tiger. Fish and forest products provide a living for up to 300,000 local families.[65]

Frontier:
3. NORTH HEILONGJIANG PROVINCE
Forest type: Boreal
Geographic location: China
Threat: Logging: 80 percent of this frontier is slated to be cut.
At risk: One of China's few remaining large intact tracts of primary forest. Habitat for several important wildlife species. Protection for the headwaters of the Amur River.

Asia has lost almost 95 percent of its frontier forests, and most of what remains is confined to the islands of Borneo, Sumatra, Sulawesi, and Irian Jaya.

THREATENED FRONTIER FORESTS OF ASIA

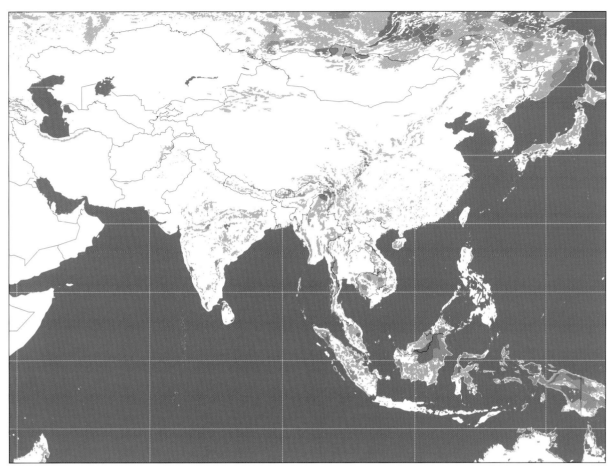

◼ **FRONTIER FORESTS UNDER LOW OR NO THREAT:** large, intact natural forest ecosystems that are relatively undisturbed and large enough to maintain all of their biodiversity.	◼ **FRONTIER FORESTS UNDER MEDIUM OR HIGH THREAT:** ongoing or planned human activities (e.g. logging, agricultural clearing, mining) will, if continued, significantly degrade these frontiers.	◻ **NON-FRONTIER FORESTS:** secondary forest, plantations, degraded forest, and patches of primary forest not meeting this study's criteria as frontier.	◼ **FRONTIER FORESTS UNASSESSED FOR THREAT:** insufficient information prevented evaluating the threat level of these frontiers.

Basemap data from ArcWorld. Assistance in data preparation, mapping and analysis provided by 🐼 World Wildlife Fund & 🌐 World Conservation Monitoring Centre.
Data sources (i.) Forest cover data provided by World Conservation Monitoring Centre. (ii.) Forest frontiers data derived through expert assessment and from other sources.

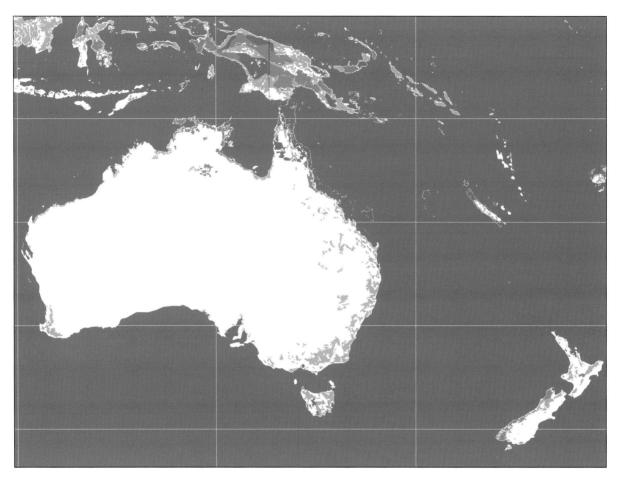

FRONTIER FORESTS UNDER LOW OR NO THREAT: large, intact natural forest ecosystems that are relatively undisturbed and large enough to maintain all of their biodiversity.

FRONTIER FORESTS UNDER MEDIUM OR HIGH THREAT: ongoing or planned human activities (e.g. logging, agricultural clearing, mining) will, if continued, significantly degrade these frontiers.

NON-FRONTIER FORESTS: secondary forest, plantations, degraded forest, and patches of primary forest not meeting this study's criteria as frontier.

FRONTIER FORESTS UNASSESSED FOR THREAT: insufficient information prevented evaluating the threat level of these frontiers.

Basemap data from ArcWorld. Assistance in data preparation, mapping and analysis provided by World Wildlife Fund & World Conservation Monitoring Centre. Data sources (i.) Forest cover data provided by World Conservation Monitoring Centre. (ii.) Forest frontiers data derived through expert assessment and from other sources.

A high percentage of Australia's native species live nowhere else on Earth.

OCEANIA (PAPUA NEW GUINEA, AUSTRALIA, AND NEW ZEALAND):

Oceania has lost almost 80 percent of its frontier forests. About three quarters of what remains is under moderate or high threat. Within the region, the status of forests varies greatly by country and forest type.

New Zealand has lost the highest percentage of frontier forest: less than 10 percent of its original forest cover remains as a frontier. Colonized by the Maori about a thousand years ago, these forests were the last of the world's large land areas to be settled by humans, but clearing for agriculture has destroyed about two thirds of all frontier forests since that date, and another 5 percent or so has been converted to plantations. Although most of New Zealand's remaining frontiers are legally protected, all are threatened by introduced species, such as the Australian brush-tailed possum, which are taking a heavy toll on the nation's endemic flora.[66,67]

A high percentage of Australia's native species live nowhere else on Earth, and much of this biodiversity resides within the nation's forests. To date, the continent has lost more than 80 percent of its original frontier forest, including large areas of species-rich, unique forest types. Three-fourths of Australia's tropical rainforest, for example, has been cleared since the late 1700s.[68]

Australia's remaining frontier forests are confined largely to Tasmania, Cape York, and the northwestern region.[69] Grazing by feral and domestic animals poses a major threat, and fire management practices are also a major concern in some areas. Logging's toll within many non-frontier areas is a serious problem. Temperate rainforests, now largely fragmented, are still cut in Tasmania and southeastern Australia — fodder for woodchips for export to Japan, which converts them into paper, packaging materials, and other products.[70,71]

Papua New Guinea (PNG) still possesses large areas of intact tropical forest — 40 percent of its original forest. Along with neighboring Irian Jaya, PNG is considered a global "biodiversity hotspot." The country probably contains at least 5 percent of the world's species within less than 1 percent of its land area.[72]

About 85 percent of PNG's frontier forests are under moderate or high threat, primarily from logging, agricultural clearing, and mining. One legacy of large clear-felling operations is soil erosion. Sediment washed by rivers to the sea threatens PNG's species-rich coral reefs and coastal fisheries.

THREATENED FRONTIERS INCLUDE:

Frontier:
1. CENTRAL NORTH ISLAND (KAWEKA/RUAHINE RANGE)
Forest type: Temperate
Geographic location: New Zealand
Threat: Introduced species (Australian brush-tailed possum and feral horses)
At risk: A high concentration of indigenous species, as well as a globally unique forest ecosystem with great biodiversity, recreational, and scenic value.

Frontier:
2. WESTERN AND GULF PROVINCES
Forest type: Tropical
Geographic location: Papua New Guinea
Threats: Logging and pipeline development. (A large oilfield has been discovered about 180 miles inland.)
At risk: A vast tract of relatively undisturbed tropical forest of exceptionally high species richness. Homelands for several groups of indigenous people.

THE CLOSING FRONTIER: A CALL TO ACTION

The news is not all bad. The opportunity to protect a priceless natural inheritance for ourselves and future generations is still ours.

his assessment found that few large intact forest ecosystems are left on the planet, and that many of these last frontiers are threatened by logging, agricultural clearing, and other activities. But the news is not all bad: even after thousands of years of forest clearing and degradation, some frontier forests remain. The opportunity to protect a priceless natural inheritance for ourselves and future generations is still ours.

But this assessment also suggests that unless we take action quickly, this opportunity is likely to pass. Against a backdrop of population growth and mounting human needs, preventing further frontier losses will require a new and balanced approach to forest management – one that protects forests' biodiversity and other assets while simultaneously providing for people and ecosystem services.

FIGURE 7

Stewardship Options for Managing Frontier Forests

OPTION ONE

■ Maintain the entire frontier forest as a protected park or reserve.
■ Develop sustainable land-use practices in surrounding non-frontier forest so that this forest serves as a buffer zone.
■ Retain biodiversity, carbon balances, and watershed quality as they are now.

OPTION TWO

■ Establish protected areas where needed within large portions of the frontier forest to preserve biodiversity.
■ Connect these areas with corridors or bridges of land that remain in natural, intact forest.
■ Introduce sustainable forest-use practices in the remaining frontier forest, whether timber extraction, hunting, tourism and ecotourism, fishing, bioprospecting, or the gathering of traditional medicinal and ritual items of value to local communities.
■ Ensure the maintenance of biodiversity, retention of carbon, and watershed protection.

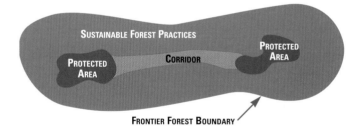

4 RESTORING FRONTIER FOREST: THE GUANACASTE EXAMPLE

Even a degraded and fragmented once-frontier forest invaded by exotic species may not necessarily be gone forever: scientists practicing restoration ecology are developing techniques to regrow native forests.

One of the world's most ambitious – and thus far successful – forest restoration efforts is in northwestern Costa Rica, where local, national, and international researchers are together restoring a

large tract of tropical dry forest in Guanacaste Conservation Area. [73]

Launched in the mid-1980s, the project features a three-pronged approach.

First, participants kicked off an aggressive fire-control program to stop human-caused fires, which were encouraging the growth of exotic grasses in cleared forest areas and killing native seedlings. Once fires were stopped, scientists allowed

wind and animals to carry in native tree seeds from an adjacent national park, helping nature when there was money by planting typical species in appropriate places and combinations. They brought in cattle to help control the grasses.

Today, the incidence of fire in Guanacaste is down 90 percent, and the introduced grass, jaragua, is virtually gone from the area. Thickets of 10- to 15-foot native trees now

dominate the landscape. Within 20 to 50 years, researchers expect the canopy to close, killing off all remaining jaragua and stopping set fires completely. They also hope that by then the forest will house viable populations of all the plant and animal species that once inhabited the area. [74]

A stewardship approach to forest management would achieve such badly needed balance. *(See Box 5.)* Such an approach should, in fact, be applied to all of the world's forests because non-frontier forests also provide humans with a range of important functions and many are high conservation priorities. Stewardship will mean pursuing different options in different parts of the world. Where few large, intact forest ecosystems remain — in temperate regions, for example — frontier forests should be largely protected in parks or reserves. Where human needs are pressing and where very large tracts of frontier forest remain,

careful development is still an option if ecologically viable core areas of forest are protected and surrounding lands managed sustainably. *(See Figure 7.)* Activities such as logging should cause minimal environmental damage and return maximum economic benefits to local people. Figure 7 illustrates how various development activities can be balanced.

How much frontier forest does the world need? At a minimum, we must maintain representative samples of all types of forest ecosystems. There are no substitutes for living examples of how each system functions or for refuges for most of the world's forest species.

As "insurance," we recommend that nations:

- Maintain more than one tract of each ecosystem type.
- Protect frontiers even when neighboring countries maintain ecologically similar forests.
- Manage land outside protected areas in ways that protect the ecological integrity of forest frontiers; and
- Try to restore fragmented and degraded forests. *(See Box 4.)*

If forest management is to reflect the needs of all, successful stewardship must include the active participation of these and other stakeholders.

NATIONAL AND LOCAL GOVERNMENTS:

Government policies must promote economic development without destroying the resource base and the environmental services provided by forests. Specifically, they should:

- Immediately halt further loss of frontier forests and restore degraded forests;
- Expand and better manage protected area systems;
- Create incentives for the private sector to manage frontier forests sustainably;
- Monitor forest quality to measure the success of management programs; and
- Encourage stewardship and educate the public about frontier forests.

---

5   A NEW VISION OF FRONTIER FOREST STEWARDSHIP

Forest management based on stewardship should include:

- Collecting all relevant information on forests and how they are being used and making it readily available to anyone with a stake in forests;
- Managing forests for long-term economic and other benefits and involving stakeholders and the public in forest-management decisions;

- Charging fees for using public forest lands and returning revenues to both the nation and local communities;
- Designing and enforcing fee regulations that discourage corruption and wasteful use of forests for short-term gain;
- Developing balanced land-use plans that set aside portions of forests for tourism, biodiversity conservation, and watershed protection;

- Attracting investors interested in using forests sustainably and making their continued access to forests contingent upon their environmental and social record;
- Including an unambiguous role for government in all large-scale forest development plans — including authority to ensure equitable distribution of revenues and long-term ecosystem viability;

- Developing capacity in public, private, or non-governmental forest agencies to plan, negotiate, implement, monitor, and enforce forest-management agreements; and
- Setting aside and conserving special forested areas in well-delineated national parks, indigenous reserves, or other protected areas.

NATIONAL AND INTERNATIONAL DONOR ORGANIZATIONS:

To promote the survival of global treasures that also provide significant environmental benefits – including carbon storage and biodiversity protection, donors should:

- Increase support for forest-rich countries, particularly neglected ones;
- Coordinate efforts among donors to maximize impact;
- Form partnerships among organizations – including the private sector – working toward forest stewardship; and
- Support projects that promote both conservation and the sustainable use of frontier forests.

BUSINESS AND THE PRIVATE SECTOR:

Traditionally viewed as enemies of conservation, private industry – from logging, mining, and oil companies to trade and retail industries – can become an agent of sound forest management if it is willing to protect jobs and cultivate long-term profits by:

- Working with non-governmental organizations, governments, and others to develop markets for products from well-managed forests;
- Avoiding investments in projects that degrade or destroy frontier forests; and
- Lobbying and encouraging governments to try policies that promote forest stewardship.

CITIZENS:

As voters and consumers partly responsible for the fate of the world's last large intact forests, citizens should:

- Ensure that decision-makers manage forests with the general public's needs in mind (at least in countries where citizens have voting power and can directly influence their leaders);
- Keep informed about policy issues affecting frontier forests; and
- Voice their concerns – through protests and boycotts, if necessary – when governments mismanage these forests.

Especially within wealthy countries, consumers can create demand for products that come from well-managed forests if they:

- Purchase only wood, paper, and other forest products that are independently certified as sustainably harvested; [75]
- Demand that retailers make such products available; and
- Reduce pressure on frontier forests by recycling and limiting consumption – not only of wood and paper, but also of energy and mineral resources from forested regions.

FRONTIER PEOPLES:

People who live within and near the world's last frontier forests stand to lose the most if these ecosystems are destroyed. Managing forests for non-timber products, ecotourism, or even sustainable logging and other resource extraction could both protect these forests and provide local income now and for future generations. As on-the-spot forest stewards, local populations should demand that the government and private sector provide opportunities for long-term economic and cultural security without environmental destruction.

NON-GOVERNMENTAL ORGANIZATIONS, INCLUDING ADVOCACY GROUPS:

Non-governmental organizations (NGOs) can mobilize critical support for conservation and stewardship. Information is one of their most powerful tools. By assessing and monitoring forest health and use, for example, NGOs can uncover evidence that governments, private industry, or others are mismanaging forests – or for that matter, doing their jobs. These organizations also should collect and disseminate information on forest stewardship in practice. Given limited time and financial resources, NGOs must coordinate their efforts and form partnerships with government agencies and private businesses.

---

6   PLAN PILOTO: SUSTAINABLE FOREST DEVELOPMENT

In Mexico's state of Quintana Roo, an organization of 16 communal groups, or ejidos, is managing 360,000 hectares of subtropical moist forest to benefit their members and, at the same time, maintain the forest. [76,77] Of the total forest area, 150,000 hectares are set aside for permanent production, primarily of mahogany and cedar. After negotiating with logging companies, participants – 3,000 as of 1991 – began to process logs, which adds value to their product and brings communities more income than shipping out raw timber does.

Before ejidos managed the forest, local communities derived no benefits from logging operations. Now, participants are working to maintain the natural forest by cutting trees on a 25-year cycle, allowing native species to regenerate, and increasing the proportion of mahogany and cedar through enrichment planting. After eight years, communities already are seeing good regeneration of natural forest – along with an income, an incentive to keep up the good work. [78]

TECHNICAL ANNEX

METHODOLOGY:

CURRENT FOREST COVER:

WRI used the only existing global map of current forest cover – that produced by the World Conservation Monitoring Centre (WCMC) in 1996, in collaboration with the World Wildlife Fund and CIFOR – as a base coverage for this assessment. The sources for this map include many country and regional maps derived from national and international sources, mostly accurate to a 1:1,000,000 scale. (All coverages used in the Frontier Forest Assessment were degraded to a 1:8,000,000 scale.) The quality, accuracy and dates of these national and regional maps vary. For details, please refer to:

The World Conservation Monitoring Centre, *The World Forest Map*, (WCMC, Cambridge, 1996).

MAPPING OF FRONTIER FOREST AREAS:

The frontier forest maps within this report reflect the knowledge and input of more than 90 experts and reviewers from around the world. Work on the Last Frontier Forests assessment began in May 1996, when WRI hosted meetings and review sessions (in Washington, Cambridge, U.K, and Rome) at which outside experts were asked to help define frontier areas and propose a methodology for mapping them. Mapping itself was a three-step process:

1. WRI first developed regional maps of "candidate frontier areas" by overlaying – using a Geographic information System (GIS) – the World Conservation Monitoring Centre's current closed forest cover map with Sierra Club's "wilderness areas" map [79] to define large wooded blocks devoid of human infrastructure (roads, settlements, etc.) where near-pristine forest might be found;

2. Approximately 90 regional forest experts were then asked to annotate these maps. Ten to fifteen individuals per region with broad knowledge of forest extent and condition reviewed the maps of candidate frontier areas and, using a checklist survey, either: (i.) nominated candidate sites as "frontier forests"; (ii.) redefined the boundaries of candidate sites or (iii.) rejected candidate sites, and;

3. WRI digitized the revised boundaries of these areas.

Experts were also asked to fill in a questionnaire for each frontier area assessed. This survey was used to build a database for each frontier site, which includes information on:

I. Forest type (based on survey results). Experts were asked to classify frontiers according to one or more of the following categories: "boreal," "temperate hardwood," "temperate mixed coniferous and deciduous forest," "southern temperate/astral forest," "humid tropical forest," "dry tropical forest."

II. Size (this was calculated using a GIS). WRI also asked experts to roughly estimate the size of each frontier assessed, where known.

III. Threats to ecosystem integrity (based on information contained within the questionnaires). Experts were asked to rank sites as under high, medium, or low threat from "commercial logging," "other biomass harvest (removal of fuelwood and construction materials, grazing)," "forest clearing (for agriculture, residential housing etc)," "road construction and other infrastructure development (e.g. powerlines, pipelines)," and "other," and to provide additional details on known threats.

iv. Potential threats to ecosystem integrity (also based on information from the questionnaires). Experts were asked to: (i.) note where significant portions of a frontier site have been allocated for current or future harvest (e.g. zoned as production forest, given over to concessions) and to estimate the percentage of each site allocated for harvest, where known; and (ii.) indicate if a site contains high-value timber species, or other high-value resources (e.g. gold, oil), and to estimate the approximate proportion of the site within which such resources occur.

v. Source of expert information and level of knowledge (for most sites, based on the input of several reviewers). The names of these individuals are listed within WRI's database, along with a ranking of how well these experts claim to know each frontier area (experts were asked to rank themselves on a 1-5 scale according to how well they know a given site).

In many cases, sites were nominated and reviewed independently by several experts. WRI harmonized these results by: (i.) consulting with reviewers when their results differed for a given site to come up with a consensus view; (ii.) in some cases, giving extra weight to results from individuals who ranked their knowledge of a site as significantly higher than that of others who reviewed that frontier forest.

WRI also held three review sessions (one covering temperate and boreal regions, a second covering tropical frontiers, and a third to review all areas of the world) to help fill in data gaps and to solicit input on draft frontier maps. Approximately 60 ecologists, foresters, and others with broad knowledge of forest issues across various regions of the globe attended these sessions.

Note that five frontier forest sites within Western Zaire were identified using maps of current road and forest cover (the latter derived from recent satellite imagery). These sites – lacking roads, or significant areas of degraded forest – were added because experts working on the WRI study suggested forest in this region qualified as "frontier," however they were not sufficiently familiar with the area to identify the boundaries of these sites.

MAPPING OF ORIGINAL FOREST COVER:
As part of this project, WCMC developed the first detailed map of estimated forest cover "prior to the impact of modern man" (circa 8,000 years ago), using many global and regional biogeographic maps. These included *World Map of Present Day Landscapes* (Moscow State University/UNEP), *Ecoregions of Latin America and the Caribbean* (Dinerstein et al.), *Vegetation of Africa* (White), *Review of the Indomalayan Protected Areas* (MacKinnon), *Australia Natural Vegetation* (Australian Surveying and Land Information Group), and *General Map of Natural Vegetation for Europe* (Bohn and Katenina). WRI adjusted this map – notably by using current forest cover in the northernmost 200 km of forest as a surrogate for historic cover so as to capture the natural patchy distribution of forest in this tundra-forest transition zone.

The WCMC map is an indicator, not a direct measure of original cover. It depicts where forest might be expected to occur today in the absence of humans, based on climate, topography, and other variables. The distribution of forest cover 8,000 years ago probably varied somewhat from region to region, due to long-term climate change. For details on the original forest cover mapping methodology, please refer to:

Clare Billington, Valerie Kapos, Mary Edwards, Simon Blyth and Susan Iremonger, *Estimated Original Forest Cover Map – A First Attempt* (WCMC, Cambridge, UK, October 1996).

FRONTIER FOREST INDEX:

The frontier forest index ranks countries on a scale of 0 to 99. The index was created by multiplying the percentage of original frontier forest lost (that estimated to cover the country 8,000 years ago) with the percentage of remaining frontier forest area classified under moderate or high threat to total assessed frontier area.

DEFINITIONS:

CURRENT FOREST COVER: estimated closed forest cover within the last 10 years or so (this date varies by country). Only closed moist forest is depicted for tropical Africa and Asia. Woodlands and shrublands are not included in this category. ORIGINAL FOREST COVER: is the estimated extent of closed forest about 8,000 years ago, assuming current climatic conditions. FRONTIER FORESTS: are defined as being primarily forested; of sufficient size to support viable populations of the full range of indigenous species associated with that particular forest ecosystem given periodic natural disturbance episodes (fire, hurricanes, pests & disease, etc.), (note that this implies that frontier forests provide habitat for these species, not that they actually contain these species); and exhibiting a structure and composition shaped largely by natural events, as well as by limited human disturbance from traditional activities (such as shifting cultivation). De facto they are relatively unmanaged (natural disturbance regimes such as fire are permitted to occur), are home to most if not all of the species associated with that ecosystem type, are dominated by indigenous tree species associated with that ecosystem type, and are characterized by mosaics of forest patches representing a range of seral stages, in areas where such landscape heterogeneity would be expected to occur under natural conditions.

Forested areas must meet all of the following 7 criteria to qualify as frontiers. They must:

1. Be of sufficient size to support ecologically viable populations of the largest carnivores and herbivores associated with that particular forest ecosystem, although they may not actually contain these species.

(*Rationale*: range requirements of umbrella species are believed to be large enough to provide for habitat requirements of most other species within a given ecosystem).

2. Be of sufficient size to support ecologically viable populations of these species in the face of a major natural disturbance episode such as one would predict to occur once in a century, within the ecosystem in question (fire, hurricanes, pests & disease, etc.).

(*Rationale*: If frontiers are supposed to serve as forest refugia during the next extinction crises, they must be large enough to maintain their resident species in the face of periodic natural disturbance. The "once in a century" cutoff, although arbitrary, is a yardstick used by engineers and others in designing bridges, buildings, dams etc. that can weather catastrophic natural events.)

3. Exhibit a structure and composition shaped largely by natural events, as well as by limited human disturbance from traditional activities (such as shifting cultivation).

4. Be relatively unmanaged (natural disturbance regimes such as fire are permitted to occur across most of the area in question).

5. Be characterized by mosaics of forest patches representing a range of seral stages, in areas where such landscape heterogeneity would be expected to occur under natural conditions.

6. Be home to most if not all of the species associated with that ecosystem type.

7. Be dominated by indigenous tree species associated with that ecosystem type.

Many temperate frontier forests do not strictly qualify according to all seven criteria, primarily due to size constraints and to fire suppression and other management. For example, Clayquot Sound in British Columbia may be too small to qualify as a frontier forest, and all sites in Scandinavia may be too disturbed to meet WRI criteria. After consultation with temperate experts we decided to include those temperate areas:(i). that are large enough to maintain ecologically viable populations of indigenous species when the surrounding non-frontier forest matrix is

considered; and: (ii.) where fires are generally allowed to burn across at least half of the frontier site (although fire suppression may have been practiced in the past). Most temperate sites in North America and Europe consist of a mix of old growth and secondary forest. Frontier sites that would not otherwise qualify using a strict interpretation of the WRI criteria are automatically listed as threatened due to lack of buffering capacity and disturbance of surrounding forest.

THREATENED FRONTIER FORESTS: are areas assessed by experts as under "medium" or "high" threat, where ongoing or planned human activities will likely result in the eventual violation of one of the seven frontier forest criteria listed above (e.g. cause declines in or local extinctions of plants and animals or large-scale changes in the forest's age and structure). In some cases, sites listed as threatened are currently undisturbed but are slated for logging or other development activity, likely to affect the ecosystem integrity of the forest. Note that many threatened frontier forests include large areas of protected forest. While the core areas of these sites may be undisturbed, these frontiers are considered threatened because human activity in surrounding forest is likely to impact the integrity of the ecosystem as a whole.

DATA CAVEATS AND LIMITATIONS

This assessment represents a rough, first-cut attempt to estimate the status of global frontier areas, and should be viewed as a work in progress. The maps and data contained within this report are not intended to be used to define conservation or investment priorities, or to otherwise provide input into regional or national planning and assessment activities. WRI will work with data partners over coming years to improve on the base maps and the accuracy of these results. Readers should note that:

■ Data availability and quality varies between regions. For example, frontier forest is likely underestimated in Central Zaire and possibly portions of Brazil, due to the fact that few scientists have explored that region (and therefore that the status of these forests is relatively unknown).

■ Naturally-fragmented forest ecosystems, such as areas of montane forest cover found in portions of East Africa, do not register as frontier forest in this study due to their small size. However, in some cases these areas may fully qualify as intact, relatively undisturbed natural forests.

■ Comparability of results has been effected by expert bias. Map reviewers varied in how strictly or loosely they have applied our criteria in defining sites and how they assessed the magnitude of any given threat. As noted above, WRI attempted to minimize this bias by seeking input from at least 10-15 experts for any one part of the world (to cross-check on and harmonize results), and by seeking extensive outside review of the draft maps to insure that data are relatively comparable between regions.

WRI would welcome any comments on the accuracy of these results and suggestions on how we might improve on the base maps during the next phase of this research project.

NOTES

1 Food and Agriculture Organization of the United Nations (FAO), Forest Resources Assessment 1990: Global Synthesis, FAO Forestry Paper 124 (FAO, Rome, 1995), Annex 1, p. 21.

2 The FAO estimate applies to annual loss of natural forest cover between 1980 and 1990 for developing countries only. It does not include large areas of forest logged over and left to regenerate. No data are available for developed countries of the world.

3 J.M. Thiollay, "Area Requirements for the Conservation of Rain Forest Raptors and Game Birds in French Guiana." *Conservation Biology*, 1989, Vol. 3(2): 128-37.

4 William Newmark, "A Land-bridge Island Perspective on Mammalian Extinctions in Western North American Parks." *Nature*, 1987, Vol 229: 430-32.

5 Christine Schonewald-Cox, "Conclusions: Guidelines to Management: A Beginning Attempt," in *Genetics and Conservation: a Reference for Managing Wild Animal and Plant Populations*, edited by Christine Schonewald-Cox, Steven Chamber, Bruce MacBryde and Larry Thomas, (London: The Benjamin/Cummings Publishing Company, Inc., 1983), pp. 415-16, 443-44.

6 Larry Harris, *The Fragmented Forest: Island Biogeography Theory and the Preservation of Biotic Diversity*, (Chicago: The University of Chicago Press, 1984), pp. 72-84.

7 Scott Robinson, Frank Thompson, Therese Donovan, Donald Whitehead and John Faaborg, "Regional Forest Fragmentation and the Nesting Success of Migratory Birds." *Science*, 1995 Vol. 267 (526): 1,987.

8 Elliot Norse, *Ancient Forests of the Pacific Northwest*, (Washington D.C.: Island Press, 1990), pp. 73, 84.

9 Walter V. Reid and Kenton Miller, *Keeping Options Alive: The Scientific Basis for Conserving Biodiversity*, (Washington, D.C.: World Resources Institute, 1989), p. 15.

10 Calculated by multiplying regional frontier forest area by per hectare carbon estimates for forest areas, presented in R.K. Dixon, S. Brown, R.A. Houghton, A.M. Solomon, M.C. Trexler and J. Wisniewski, "Carbon Pools and Flux of Global Forest Ecosystems." *Science*, Vol. 263: 185-90. Dixon et al's estimates are for closed and open forests for both soil and above-ground vegetation. For this reason, and because these averages include degraded forest (which contains less carbon than intact forest) the figure presented in the text on total carbon stored in frontier forest is likely an underestimate. Soil carbon figures include peat. We used averaged per hectare carbon figures in estimating carbon stored in frontier forests that contain more than one dominant forest type (e.g. temperate and boreal forest).

11 John Perlin, *A Forest Journey: The Role of Wood in the Development of Civilization*, (New York: W.W. Norton and Company, 1989), pp. 18-19, 42-43.

12 World Resources Institute, World Resources 1992-93, (New York: Oxford University Press, 1992), p. 290.

13 George Ledec and Robert Goodland, *Wildlands: Their Protection and Management in Economic Development*, (Washington, D.C.: The World Bank, 1988), pp. 26-7.

14 Nels Johnson and Bruce Cabarle, *Surviving the Cut: Natural Forest Management in the Humid Tropics*, (Washington, D.C.: World Resources Institute, 1993) p. 7.

15 Commission on Development and Environment for Amazonia, *Amazonia Without Myths*, Amazon Cooperation Treaty, 1992. p. xiv.

16 Food and Agriculture Organization of the United Nations (FAO), Forest Resources Assessment 1990: Global Synthesis, FAO Forestry Paper 124, (Rome: FAO, 1995), p. 43.

17 K.D. Singh, personal communication, January 1997; *Washington Post*, January 1, 1997.

18 United States Department of Commerce, *Statistical Abstract of the United States 1996*, (Washington: United States Department of Commerce, 1996), pp. 8, 562.

19 This study was limited to mapping frontier forests within closed forest ecosystems. WRI was unable to map large natural tracts of woodland area (more open forest, generally located in drier regions of the world, between closed forest and savannah), because no global map exists depicting wooded areas of the world.

20 Geographic Information Systems are used to store, analyze and display spatially-referenced (map) data.

21 United Nations Environment Programme (UNEP), *Global Biodiversity Assessment*, (Cambridge, Cambridge University Press, 1995), p. 345.

22 Alexander Mather, *Global Forest Resources*, (Portland: Timber Press, 1990), p. 32.

23 Jack Westoby, *Introduction to World Forestry*, (Oxford: Basil Blackwell Ltd., 1989), p. 50.

24 Jack Westoby, *Introduction to World Forestry*, (Oxford: Basil Blackwell Ltd., 1989), pp. 54-5.

25 Owen Lynch and Kirk Talbott, *Balancing Acts: Community-Based Forest Management and National Law in Asia and the Pacific*, (Washington, D.C.: World Resources Institute, 1995), p. 21.

26 Commission on Development and Environment for Amazonia, *Amazonia Without Myths*, Amazon Cooperation Treaty, 1992, p. xii.

27 R. B. Edgerton, *Sick Societies: Challenging the Myth of Primitive Harmony*, (New York: Free Press, 1992).

28 United Nations Environment Programme (UNEP), *Global Biodiversity Assessment*, (Cambridge: Cambridge University Press, 1995), p. 765.

29 Duncan Poore, Peter Burgess, John Palmer, Simon Rietburgen and Timothy Synnott, *No Timber Without Trees: Sustainability in the Tropical Forest*, (London: Earthscan Publications, 1989), p. 18.

30 Consultative Group on International Agricultural Research (CGIAR), *Poor Farmers Could Destroy Half of Remaining Tropical Forest*, media backgrounder to press release, (Washington, D.C.: CGIAR; August 4, 1996), p. 3.

31 Raymond Rowe, Narendra Sharma and John Browder, "Deforestation: Problems, Causes and Concerns," in *Managing the World's Forests*, Narendra Sharma, ed., (Dubuque, Iowa: Kendall/Hunt Publishing Company, 1992), p. 34.

32 International Panel on Climate Change (IPCC), *IPCC Working Group II Second Assessment Report*, (IPCC, 1995).

33 World Resources Institute, *World Resources 1996-97*, (New York: Oxford University Press, 1996), p. 190.

34 Global Witness, *Corruption, War and Forest Policy: The Unsustainable Exploitation of Cambodia's Forests*, (London: Global Witness Ltd., February 1996) p. 3.

35 Kirk Talbott and Chantal Elkin, *Logging Burma's Forests: Resources for the Regime*, (Washington, D.C.: World Resources Institute, forthcoming).

36 Environmental Investigation Agency (EIA), *Corporate Power, Corruption and the Destruction of the World's Forests: The Case for a New Global Forest Agreement*, (Washington, D.C.: EIA, 1995), pp. 6-7.

37 Nigel Sizer and Richard Rice, *Backs to the Wall in Suriname: Forest Policy in a Country in Crisis*, (Washington, D.C.: World Resources Institute, 1995), p. 11.

38 World Press Review, "Colombia's Vanishing Forests," *World Press Review*, Vol. 40, No. 6, June 1993, p. 34.

39 Nigel Smith, Paulo Alvim, Emanuel Serrao, and Italo Falesi, "Amazonia," in *Regions at Risk: Comparisons of Threatened Environments*, Jeanne Kasperson, Roger Kasperson and B. L. Turner II, eds., (Tokyo: United Nations University Press, 1995), pp. 58-9.

40 Ecotrust and Conservation International (CI), *Coastal Temperate Rain Forests: Ecological Characteristics, Status and Distribution Worldwide,* Occasional Paper Series No. 1, (Portland: Ecotrust, 1992), p. 33.

41 Jonathan Friedland and Raphael Pura, "Log Heaven: Trouble at Home, Asian Timber Firms Set Sights on the Amazon," *The Wall Street Journal,* November 11, 1996.

42 World Wildlife Fund, *The Official World Wildlife Fund Guide to Endangered Species of North America,* (Washington: Beacham Publishing Inc., 1990), pp. 446, 534, 549.

43 Development and degradation of surrounding non-protected forest area threatens the ecological integrity of these sites, which barely qualified as frontier forest under the WRI criteria. Refer to Technical Annex for details.

44 Chuck Carr, personal communication, 1996.

45 Robin Hanbury-Tension, "A Bridge Too Far?," *Geographical Magazine,* Vol. 68, No. 1, January 1996, p. 35.

46 Food and Agriculture Organization of the United Nations (FAO), *Forest Resources Assessment 1990: Global Synthesis,* FAO Forestry Paper 124, (Rome: FAO, 1995), Annex 1, p. 21.

47 The Guyana Shield includes part or all of Brazil, French Guiana, Guyana, Suriname, and Venezuela.

48 Peter Raven, personal communication, December 1996.

49 Nigel Smith, Paulo Alvim, Emanuel Serrao, and Italo Falesi, "Amazonia," in *Regions at Risk: Comparisons of Threatened Environments,* Jeanne Kasperson, Roger Kasperson and B. L. Turner II, eds., (Tokyo: United Nations University Press, 1995), p. 41.

50 Caroline Harcourt and Jeffrey Sayer, eds, *The Conservation Atlas of Tropical Forests: the Americas,* (New York: Simon and Schuster, 1996), pp. 230, 238.

51 M. Patricia Marchak, *Logging the Globe,* (London: McGill-Queen's University Press, 1995), p. 321.

52 Steve Gilroy, "Disturbing the Ancients," in *Buzzworm: The Environmental Journal,* Vol. IX, No. 1, January/February 1992, p. 41.

53 Nigel Dudley, *Forests in Trouble: A Review of the Status of Temperate Forests Worldwide,* (Gland, Switzerland: World Wildlife Fund, 1992), p. 121.

54 Steve Gilroy, "Disturbing the Ancients," in *Buzzworm: The Environmental Journal,* Vol. IX, No. 1, January/February 1992, p. 38.

55 Estimate of the proportion of the Congo Basin's forest cover located in Zaire is based on figures in: Food and Agriculture Organization of the United Nations (FAO), *Forest Resources Assessment 1990: Global Synthesis,* FAO Forestry Paper 124 (Rome: FAO, 1995), Annex 1, p. 28.

56 Food and Agriculture Organization of the United Nations (FAO), *Forest Resources Assessment 1990: Tropical Countries,* FAO Forestry Paper 112, (Rome: FAO, 1993), Annex 1, Table 5a.

57 World Resources Institute, *World Resources 1996-97,* (New York: Oxford University Press, 1996), p. 210.

58 World Resources Institute, *World Resources 1996-97,* (New York: Oxford University Press, 1996), pp. 206, 218.

59 Josh Newell and Emma Wilson, *The Russian Far East: Forests, Biodiversity Hotspots and Industrial Developments,* (Tokyo: Friends of the Earth-Japan, 1996), pp. 6, 46.

60 World Resources Institute, *World Resources 1996-97,* (New York: Oxford University Press, 1996), pp. 206-7.

61 Josh Newell and Emma Wilson, *The Russian Far East: Forests, Biodiversity Hotspots and Industrial Developments,* (Tokyo: Friends of the Earth-Japan, 1996), pp. 46, 53.

62 K.D. Singh and Antonio Marzoli, "Deforestation Trends in the Tropics: A Time Series Analysis," paper presented at the World Wildlife Fund Conference on Potential Impact of Climate Change on Tropical Forests, San Juan, Puerto Rico, April 1995, pp. 8-9.

63 National Development Planning Agency, Government of Indonesia, *Sixth Five-Year Development Plan 1994/5-1998/9,* Vol. III, (Jakarta: National Planning Agency, 1994), pp. 421-22.

64 World Resources Institute, *World Resources 1996-97,* (New York: Oxford University Press, 1996), pp. 191, 217.

65 World Resources Institute, *Bangladesh: Environment and Natural Resource Assessment,* (Washington, D.C.: World Resources Institute, 1990), p. 27.

66 World Wide Fund for Nature (WWF) and the World Conservation Union (IUCN), *Centres of Plant Diversity: A Guide and Strategy for their Conservation,* Vol. II, (Cambridge: WWF, 1995), p. 449.

67 New Zealand Ministry for the Environment, *New Zealand's National Report to the United Nations Conference on Environment and Development,* (Wellington: Ministry for the Environment, 1991), pp. 47-8.

68 World Wide Fund for Nature (WWF) and the World Conservation Union (IUCN), *Centres of Plant Diversity: A Guide and Strategy for their Conservation,* Vol. II, (Cambridge: WWF, 1995), p. 439.

69 Frontier forests in Northern Australia contain a mix of forest and woodland, including small patches of rainforest.

70 Mark Clayton, "Chipping Away at Australia's Old-Growth Forests," *The Christian Science Monitor,* April 24, 1996.

71 Nigel Dudley, *Forests in Trouble: A Review of the Status of Temperate Forests Worldwide,* (Gland, Switzerland: World Wildlife Fund, 1992), pp. 93-5.

72 Department of Environment and Conservation, Conservation Resource Centre, and the Africa Centre for Resources and Environment, *Papua New Guinea Country Study on Biological Diversity,* (Waigani: Department of Environment and Conservation, 1995), p. 6.

73 Such as certification efforts approved by the Forest Stewardship Council, (eg. Smartwood), which ensure that harvesting is environmentally responsible, socially beneficial (particularly to local communities), and financially viable.

74 David Tenenbaum, "The Guanacaste Idea," *American Forests,* Vol. 100, Nos. 11-12, November-December 1994, p. 28.

75 David Tenenbaum, "The Guanacaste Idea," *American Forests,* Vol. 100, Nos. 11-12, November-December 1994, p. 28.

76 Matthew Perl, Michael Kiernan, Dennis McCaffrey, Robert Buschbacher, and Garo Batmanian, *Views From the Forest: Natural Forest Management Initiatives in Latin America,* (Washington, D.C.: World Wildlife Fund, 1991), p. 5.

77 Nels Johnson and Bruce Cabarle, *Surviving the Cut: Natural Forest Management in the Humid Tropics,* (Washington D.C.: World Resources Institute, 1993) p. 28.

78 Matthew Perl, Michael Kiernan, Dennis McCaffrey, Robert Buschbacher, and Garo Batmanian, *Views From the Forest: Natural Forest Management Initiatives in Latin America,* (Washington, D.C.: World Wildlife Fund, 1991), pp. 5, 8.

79 Michael McCloskey and Heather Spalding, "A Reconnaissance-level Inventory of the Amount of Wilderness Remaining in the World," *Ambio,* Vol. 18, No. 4, 1989, pp. 221-27.

DATE DUE

			Printed in USA